THE YOUNG DEAF CHILD

David M. Luterman, D.Ed.
with
Ellen Kurtzer-White, M.S.
and
Richard C. Seewald, Ph.D.

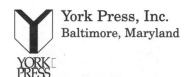

York Press, Inc.
Baltimore, Maryland

YORK
PRESS

This book was manufactured in the United States of America.
Typography by Type Shoppe II Productions Ltd.
Printing and binding by P. H. Hutchison Co., Inc.
Cover design by Joseph Dieter, Jr.

Library of Congress Cataloging-in-Publication Data
   The young deaf child / David M. Luterman : with Ellen Kurtzer
-White and Richard C. Seewald.
      p. cm.
   Includes bibliographical references and index.
   ISBN 0-912752-46-7   (paper)
   1. Deafness in children--Diagnosis.   2. Deaf children-
-Rehabilitation--Decision making.   I. Kurtzer-White, Ellen.
II. Seewald, Richard C.   III. Title
RF291.5.C45L88   1999   99-11344
618.92'0978--dc21   CIP

This book is dedicated to all those many nursery two-year olds who have grown up to become fine adults.

ACKNOWLEDGMENTS

All books are collaborative experiences, this book more so than most. In addition to the obvious collaborations of Ellen Kurtzer-White and Richard Seewald, who wrote chapters for this book, I have had help from many sources over the years. Sue Colten, Julie Goldberg, and Ellen Kurtzer-White have worked with me as supervisors in the nursery program, and have helped shape my ideas about educating children. Mark Ross is a wise counselor and friend who is always there to bounce ideas off. Liz Bezera, librarian par excellence, very often anticipates my needs, and I will probably mention her in my will. Dorothy Aram was a critical reader—one every author needs badly. Julie Goldberg and Lauren Aron read and commented on chapters. Any errors in this manuscript are mine. Elinor Hartwig, publisher of York Press, who takes very good care of her authors, has helped this one in particular. Joan Miller quickly and competently typed this manuscript, adding support and comments. Her help was invaluable. And, of course, my wife Cari has always done whatever she can to be helpful.

Contents

ix   Foreword

xv   Introduction

1   CHAPTER 1
The Methodology Wars in the United States

35   CHAPTER 2
Early Detection

55   CHAPTER 3
Programs

85   CHAPTER 4
Early Intervention: Revisiting Therapy
Ellen Kurtzer-White

149   CHAPTER 5
Assistive Hearing Technologies
Richard C. Seewald

187   CHAPTER 6
Counseling

217   References

231   Index

Foreword

Recently I received a call from very close friends who had disturbing news: they had just learned that one of their grandchildren, the first child of their youngest son, was deaf. Could I help them? What advice could I offer?

This is a child whose audiological test results indicate minimal residual hearing. Electrophysiological tests, they said, indicated that the girl has a profound, bilateral hearing loss. A powerful set of binaural behind-the-ear aids has been fitted, but the girl's prognosis is not good.

The parents are receiving well-meant, but conflicting advice. Advice has come from the hospital where the diagnosis was made, from the child's pediatrician, and from the staff (and parents) associated with two preschool programs for children with hearing impairments.

One group feels that with an intensive auditory-verbal approach she could be educated orally, with the further possibility of a cochlear implant when she reaches two years of age. The staff of the second program suggested that the child could prepare herself to enter the deaf community; she should be exposed immediately to signing (which the parents, together with much of the rest of the large, close family would be expected to learn).

What advice could I offer? From my perspective as a professional in the field of hearing disorders, I see that the family is experiencing something similar to what hundreds of parents experienced. There is nothing new about their history or their quandary. Yet, because of my close personal attachment to the family, their experiences are now new to me, and certainly very new to the parents and grandparents who had never conceived of this kind of event showing up in their lives.

I know what I would do in similar circumstances. I would elect the auditory-verbal training program with a cochlear implant later; but this is a decision that must be made by the parents, not the grandparents, not professionals, and certainly not the family friend. The family will make the decision that is right for them. Professionals must be the junior partners in making such a decision.

The target audience of the book comprises those who have diagnostic and therapeutic responsibilities for young children newly identified with hearing loss. The primary message is that the parents, for better or worse, the most important figures in their children's lives—their first "teachers." In the interests of the children, parents cannot be shunted off to a secondary role. Beyond this perception, David Luterman views the parents as people who, overwhelmed and overwrought by the shattering impact of having a deaf child, require our assistance in terms of their own needs. Our clients are not just the children but their parents as well.

Satisfying the needs and reducing the conflicts of the parents should help the children. It is important to emphasize the almost symbiotic relationship that exists between a child and his parents, most clearly with the mother. As the parents work through their own feeling regarding their child, the impact on the child cannot help but be favorable, and probably result in improvements in the child's performance. The corollary of this reasoning, of course, is that improvement in the child's performance through the appropriate selection and utilization of amplification, may lessen parental anxiety. The reciprocity of the relationship between a child and his parents is an ever-present consideration in working with families of children with hearing impairments.

No one "system" is prescribed for parent involvement, nor is any one parent-infant program, nursery program, or communication mode advocated here for all children with hearing impairments. Such an imposition on people would violate one of the basic themes permeating this book, and that is the explicit recognition of individual differences and circumstances. Dr. Luterman presents a number of models for organizing different types of programs that involve different styles and degrees of parental involvement. Although he prefers the auditory-oral mode of communication, nowhere does that preference get elevated to a religious disputation; rather, his focus remains on the child and his parents, and encompasses more fundamental concerns than the mode of communication, such as the child's psychosocial status, the relationship between the child and his or her parents, and, finally, the parents' acceptance of the reality of their child's condition.

The book conveys another important message to those readers, (mainly audiologists, educators of the deaf, or speech and language pathologists) whose professional mission requires that they provide direct and on-going therapy services to children with hearing impairments and their parents. It is a message that, in my experience, does not get much recognition by members of those groups, the associations they belong to, or the institutions that train them. Its essence is contained in the quotation "Physician, heal thyself." Dealing as we do with some of the strongest human emotions and feelings, we should recognize that the state of our own emotional well-being can warp the therapeutic relationship. We are not mechanics dealing with machines. Our own personalities, our own needs, and our own deficiencies and strengths enter into our interactions with people and thereby modify our relationships with them. The healthier we are, the more we can effectively enter the therapy process and the more likely we are that our ostensible therapy goals are the actual ones, and not just a smokescreen within which our own hidden needs get satisfied. Too often we seem to find some colleagues operating as emotional scavengers, feeding on the dependencies of their clients to fill the emotional gaps in themselves. Professional growth should imply more than the mere accumulation of data, important as the process is; it should also imply the concurrent expansion of one's emotional vision into oneself. No one I know in this field is a better example of the sentiments I am expressing than David Luterman. Although writing about an author's personal qualities as a foreword to his book may not seem to be appropriate, those personal qualities represent a good deal of what this book is all about. Listen to him speak through the words of this book; listen to his doubts, his self-examinations, his striving to understand himself, and through himself, his clients. Listen to him carefully and you will hear a therapist, in the true sense of the word—a healer—speaking to you, saying that his efforts are devoted to helping people heal themselves by helping them remove the barriers from self-actualization. We can perhaps visualize him best, and his lessons for us to emulate, as a gentle conductor, nudging his clients on the path to personal insight and growth but, at the same time, accompanying them on their path.

On a number of occasions in the past, I have had an opportunity to meet and talk to Dr. Luterman's "graduates," the parents who have completed his year-long program. They are a unique breed. Nowhere have I met parents of children with hearing impairments who demonstrated a more effective and realistic concern for the welfare of their children. There was also no lack of the information that traditional "counseling" programs emphasize, these parents were fully informed regarding language and speech development, hearing aids, and the pros and cons of different communication modes and educational placements. What distinguished them was their capacity to use that information realistically and to see its applicability to their children.

The active participation of such parents on the educational scene is an absolute necessity, more now than ever before. We are inundated with laws, regulations, and guidelines, all of which have laudable purposes, but which sometimes appear to impede rather than foster educational services and alternatives for children with hearing impairments. It is easy for the average parents, and educators as well, to be overwhelmed by the complexity of the regulations they are expected to observe. Programs and, by extension, children often are judged by their conformance to those regulations and not by educational quality or educational progress. Children are being lost in a morass of red tape; in my judgment, they can best be extracted from this predicament by the involvement of informed parents in the political process. The realization of that opportunity is a bonus consideration in programs such as Dr. Luterman's. In the long run, it may be the one that has the greatest impact for all children with hearing impairments.

The book, however, is basically not about bureaucrats, parents, children, or even professionals for that matter; it is about people who happen to wear different labels denoting a different status. For most of this book, David Luterman speaks universally to all of us, as a whole man giving us the lessons of his experiences, so that we may see ourselves more clearly and thus also see those entrusted to our care with more understanding.

This new book by David Luterman is about how to help families through this kind of crisis, with information, counseling (listening, really) and support for their own judgments as it affects their children. To round it out, Dr. Luterman has selected an experienced clinician and teacher, Ellen White, to write on "Approaches to Therapy," and Richard Seewald, an internationally acclaimed pediatric audiologist to write on the "Technology of Deafness." It doesn't get much better than this.

—Mark Ross

Introduction

In 1985, I convened a conference to celebrate the twentieth anniversary of our family-centered nursery program for hearing impaired children. The purpose of the conference was to examine and evaluate the previous twenty years of education of the deaf which, at that point, seemed to us to be especially turbulent with many exciting and revolutionary ideas emerging. The proceedings of the conference were published in a book entitled Deafness in Perspective (Luterman 1986). Little did the participants realize, nor could we anticipate that the next thirteen years would see a dwarfing of the previous twenty years' changes.

In retrospect, one can see that the seeds of our current ferment in education of the deaf were being planted in the sixties and seventies and have now borne a very strange fruit. We are living in a marvelous time that simply boggles the mind. We have made enormous technological breakthroughs that, if employed properly, can minimize the negative educational consequences of deafness: We now have the means to detect hearing loss in newborns; hearing aid design has advanced considerably so that we now have programmable "smart aids" using a digital technology that gives a clear signal and, lastly, we have cochlear implants for the very deaf which are producing a new kind of child—"the hard of hearing deaf child." There is no doubt in my mind that the current implants will be considered quite crude in a relatively few years and many of the restrictions now in place regarding prescriptions of implants will be lifted so that they will be readily available to the hearing impaired. This should further advance the opportunities for an auditory/verbal approach to educating the deaf.

Simultaneously with the advent of technological advances, the deaf community has given us the startling message that deafness is not a medical condition that requires correction, but rather a cultural difference that needs to be respected. This notion has given rise to the educational philosophy known as the bi-lingual, bi-cultural approach which states that American Sign Language (ASL) is the natural language of the deaf and should be taught first with English learned later as a second language. The use of technology in the form of hearing aids and cochlear implants is minimized and in some quarters, implants are seen as devices used to commit genocide.

We currently have an incredible juxtaposition of these two very different philosophies and approaches to childhood deafness. What is a professional working in the field of deafness and what is a parent of a newly diagnosed deaf child to do? This book is written to help the professional and, perhaps the parent, sort out these issues and make their way through the maze of competing philosophies.

Chapter one traces the history of deaf education in the United States regarding issues of methodology. It is only by understanding our origins that we can begin to appreciate our present situation. Chapter two looks at the issue of newborn screening and its implications for a good habilitation model. Chapter three describes programming for the young deaf child without recourse to any methodological issues. Chapter four, written by Ellen Kurtzer-White, examines therapy for the young deaf child and Chapter five, written by Richard Seewald, describes the amazing technology currently available for deaf children. Chapter six revisits, for me, issues in counseling parents of young deaf children. It is clear from the literature and my own clinical experience of over thirty-five years that the key to the habilitation of young deaf children is the parents, and success in deafness habilitation does not reside in methodology or technology alone. Neither our skills nor our technology are of any use unless we can communicate effectively with parents. In order to do this, we are going to need enhanced counseling skills. This chapter tries to incorporate much that I have learned in working with parents over the past thirty-three years, and is a reworking of my first book about parent counseling, written twenty years ago.

In the preface to the 1985 book, I cited an ancient Chinese curse: "May you live in interesting times." It is a curse because when you live in interesting times you cannot appreciate them. It is only from a time removed that you can gain the necessary perspective to appreciate the era in which you lived. Perhaps we cannot fully appreciate our exciting present but certainly the young deaf child approaching the millennium has many more opportunities than the child of the beginning of this century—the times are "interesting" and certainly pregnant with possibilities. If we intellectually apply all we now know, deaf children will be considerably better off in the next century than they have been in this one.

In a small way, this volume is an attempt to further the process of examining the tremendous ferment currently taking place in education of the deaf, in order to gain a new perspective on deafness.

CHAPTER I

The Methodology Wars in the United States

The history of education of the deaf is replete with methodology wars; the loser in these monumental battles has been the deaf child. In the nineteenth century there was a clear-cut battle between the oralists and the manualists. The modern 20th century equivalent is a more subtle conflict in that there are gradients in each "army," but essentially it is the same war: The oralists ardently believe that there is something wrong with a deaf child that needs fixing. Their goal is to make him or her as much like a hearing person as possible. The modern day manualist believes that the first goal of education is to have a well-adjusted deaf child who can communicate using the "natural" language (for deaf children) of signs. The code word for a manualist is "communication" and the oralist soldier can be identified by the shibboleth "normal."

The establishment of the first ongoing school for the education of deaf children in the United States is generally credited to Thomas Hopkins Gallaudet. A young theology student and graduate of Yale University, he was planning to pursue a career as a minister after abandoning his original plan of studying law because of ill health. In 1814, he became interested in the education of a neighbor's child, Alice Cogswell, then nine years old, and deaf from meningitis at age three. Her father, Dr. Mason Fitch Cogswell, a prominent surgeon in Hartford, was determined to fund a school for deaf children. He conducted a census through paid advertisements, and located 80 hearing impaired children of school age. From his data, he estimated that there should be 400 in New England, and upwards of 2,000 in the United States (Bender 1981). He presented his data to community leaders in Hartford, funds were raised, and Thomas Hopkins Gallaudet was somewhat reluctantly recruited to go to Europe to study education of the deaf, with the intention of returning to the United States to establish a school. He left in 1815, bound for England to study with the Braidwoods, the proprietors of an oral school in England. Negotiations between Gallaudet and the Braidwoods broke down, apparently because they were reluctant to reveal their methods for teaching. The Braidwoods proposed that Gallaudet spend three years at their school (Bender 1981) and that they send their own teacher to the United States. Neither proposal was suitable to Gallaudet, who, subsequently, went to France to study with the Abbe Sicard at the French school.

The French school had been established by the Abbe de L'Epee in 1779. The good Abbe had worked with two deaf sisters discovered in his parish. He evolved a formal sign system based, in part, on the gestural, untutored (i.e., "natural") language developed by the sisters. This manual language system became the basis of instruction at the school. While he did not condemn the teaching of speech by others, he felt the deaf were capable of thought and reason only by the use of signs. It was to this school and to this philosophy that

Gallaudet was heavily exposed. In June, 1816, he returned to the United States with Laurent Clerc, a deaf pupil who had graduated from the French school as an assistant teacher.

On April 15, 1817, the American Asylum for the Education of the Deaf and Dumb (now the American School for the Deaf) was established. Funding was provided by the Connecticut legislature, private foundations, and, ultimately, the Federal government (Moores 1996). The American School for the Deaf is the oldest established school in the United States and its method of instruction was ardently manualist. First, the children were taught natural signs, and then the more formal signs developed by de L'Epee. Finally, the manual alphabet was introduced which would lead to teaching written English. There was no attempt to teach speech. Manualism was firmly established in the United States at the American Asylum, and the school became the principal training ground for teachers wishing to estab lish other programs in the United States. Manual education was the prime educational modality used, and all subsequent schools for the next four decades in the United States used the manual system.

It was not until nearly forty years later that oralism established a foothold in the United States. The organizing force for the establishment of an oral school, as with the manual school, was parents. Mabel Hubbard, the daughter of Gardiner Hubbard, was deafened by scarlet fever at the age of four. The Hubbards joined forces with two other families—the Lippets and Cushings—to petition the Massachusetts Legislature for the establishment of an oral school. Horace Mann, a philanthropist interested in education, at the Hubbards' request, traveled to Europe—Germany in particular— and reported that deaf children were doing well using lip reading and speech. The parents wanted their children to speak and did not endorse the manual/nonspeaking approach of the American School. All three of the founding families employed teachers of normally hearing children as tutors, and so they were not influenced by the American School and the use of manualism in the education of the deaf (Bender 1981). Funding from the Massachusetts state legislature for an oral school was denied because of opposition from the American School which sent pupils to demonstrate the advantages of the manual system. This was the first skirmish in what was to become a monumental battle.

Hubbard, not to be defeated, persuaded Harriet Rogers, a tutor of Fanny Cushing and teacher of hearing children, to open a private oral school in 1867. The school opened with eight children, with tuition subsidized by Hubbard. The school served as a demonstration project to the public, showing the advantages of oral education. It should be noted that many of the "stars" were adventitiously deafened children and, therefore, had established some speech and language skills prior to the onset of hearing loss (Bender 1981). It is also of interest to note that there was no testing of the children's hearing, and I am sure that many of these children who were termed "deaf," had considerable residual hearing and would currently be classified as hard of hearing. Nevertheless, the school demonstrated the viability of using an oral approach (which did not rely on any signing) to educate the deaf child. In fact, signing was actively discouraged because it was thought to detract from lip-reading and learning English. John Clarke, a philanthropist, who was gradually losing his hearing, gave a grant of $50,000 to establish an oral school for the deaf in Northampton, Massachusetts. The school, nurtured by Hubbard, with

Rogers as principal, moved to Northampton and became the Clarke School for the Deaf. Now the methodology battle was to be conducted by two very able generals: Alexander Graham Bell and Edward Miner Gallaudet.

The parallels in the lives of these two men are startling. Both were brilliant, achieving success very early. Both had famous and successful fathers, and both had deaf mothers (Winefield 1987). Edward Miner Gallaudet was the youngest of twelve children born to Thomas Hopkins Gallaudet and Sophie Fowler Gallaudet, who was a deaf student and graduate of The American School. Following his father's death, the young Gallaudet, at age fourteen, worked in a bank for several years. He entered Trinity College as a junior, simultaneously working as a part-time teacher at the American School (Moores 1996). After graduating from Trinity at the age of 19, he accepted a full-time teaching position at the American School. In 1857, at the age of twenty, he was chosen to be the principal of the newly established Columbia Institute for the Deaf and Dumb in Washington DC. He was accompanied by his mother who served as matron of the school. The school was successful, later adding a collegiate department, which was the first, and for many years, the only institute of higher education for deaf students. This college received federal funding support, the name was later changed to Gallaudet College and is now a University. Although a strong advocate of sign language in the instruction of the deaf, Edward Miner Gallaudet departed from his father's views in that he also believed in teaching articulation to the deaf, and advocated the use of a simultaneous or combined method whereby both signing and speech were taught. In 1868, he convened a conference of principals of schools for the deaf with the major topic being methodology. Gallaudet forcefully argued for the use of articulation training in education. He wrote an article in 1871 (recently reprinted) that was critical of the excessive use of sign language which he believed hindered the learning of written English. He noted the large number of students who graduated and did not achieve mastery of English (Gallaudet 1997). The conference, at Gallaudet's urging, concluded that all institutions educating the Deaf had a responsibility to teach lip-reading and articulation to all students who might benefit from it. Moores (1996) credits Gallaudet with being "the father of oral education." I think this goes a bit too far; more accurately, he is the father of total communication, a method that emerged and gained educational credence nearly a century later.

Alexander Graham Bell became the father of oral education and its most ardent promoter. The second of three sons, he was born in Scotland and raised in England. His father, Melville Bell, was a noted teacher of diction, intensely interested in the improvement of speech, and probably the prototypical speech pathologist. He had an ear for dialect and was the model George Bernard Shaw used for the character of Henry Higgins in his play *Pygmalion*, later to become the musical *My Fair Lady*. Melville Bell's wife, Eliza, had lost much of her hearing during childhood, with the likelihood that her loss was severe and not profound, since she had good speech and excellent language (Winefield 1987). There is no doubt that Alexander Graham Bell's exposure to his mother as an orally communicating deaf woman, who did not rely on sign language, influenced his thinking about education of the deaf. (Conversely, it was Edward Miner Gallaudet's experience with a deaf, signing mother who influenced his thinking about education.) Bell's father, however, provided the link to education of the deaf. Melville Bell developed visible speech—a system that described speech through written symbols. He devised this method as a means for improving speech, and trained his sons to use this technique. Lecturing widely, Melville Bell suggested that this might be a method to teach the deaf. Alexander, despite his total lack of knowledge or experience in teaching deaf children, began working with two deaf pupils using visible speech (later abandoned as being too cumbersome) (Bender 1981). He reported success almost immediately and always retained an intense interest in the education of the deaf and in promoting oral instruction for the deaf. He always thought of himself as a teacher of the deaf (Bruce 1973).

Because both of Alexander's brothers died of tuberculosis, the family moved from England to Bradford, Canada, seeking a better climate. Melville Bell was invited to lecture and teach visible speech at The Boston Day School (the second established school for the deaf in Massachusetts, later to become known as The Horace Mann School). Instead, he sent Alexander who had decided to settle in the Boston area. Alexander Graham Bell opened a training school to teach visible speech, and Mabel Hubbard, a young deaf girl who was one of the first students at Clarke School, enrolled in it. They fell in love. Because Bell was trying to fashion a living by tutoring deaf students and teaching at Boston University as a professor of vocal physiology and elocution, there was neither much time nor money to conduct a courtship. The relationship was put on hold at their parents' insistence. Hubbard did financially support Bell's acoustic experimental work which culminated in the invention of the telephone, ultimately enriching both. Fancifully, it was thought that Bell was working on developing a hearing aid when he discovered the telephone. Although this is not true, components of the telephone are also parts of the wearable hearing aid developed nearly fifty years later (Bruce 1973).

Objections to the marriage were finally lifted and Bell and Mabel Hubbard were married. Their marriage was lifelong and happy (Winefield 1987). Alexander Bell, like his father before him, was to live with a successful, orally trained woman.

Bell and Gallaudet started as friends but swiftly became rivals for the leadership in education of the deaf. In 1890, Bell founded the American Association for Teaching Speech to the Deaf. This developed into a national organization to promote oralism; and, in effect, split from the Convention of American Instructors of the Deaf, Gallaudet's organization. In two published papers, as reported by Moores (1996), Bell's stated position was basically that the American system of educating the deaf in residential schools with a heavy emphasis on signing only led to isolating the deaf and promoting intermarriage of the deaf with the resultant birth of more deaf children. This position was consistent with the eugenics movement then emerging, which had the mistaken notion that recessive genes could be eliminated by not allowing intramarriage of the carriers of the gene.

Through oralism and educating deaf children with hearing students, Bell hoped to "eliminate the formation of a deaf race" by promoting marriages between hearing and deaf individuals—an interesting position for a man whose mother and wife were both deaf. He favored the elimination of educational segregation, of the use of sign language, and of the use of deaf teachers of deaf children. (At that point over one third of all teachers in schools for the deaf were themselves deaf, following the example of Clerc, the first teacher at the American School).

Edward Miner Gallaudet strongly opposed these positions, and the two men vigorously debated each other at professional meetings. The culmination of their animosity occurred when Gallaudet wished to establish a teacher training program at Columbia College and sought funding from the Federal legislature. Bell opposed funding the program, fearful that Gallaudet would employ deaf teachers and use sign language. Bell effectively sabotaged the appropriation and Gallaudet never forgave him. When Bell later attempted to join the Convention of American Instructors of the Deaf, when Gallaudet was president, his money was refused. The split was permanent and wide (Winefield 1987).

In 1880, an international congress on education of the deaf was covened. Both Gallaudet and Bell attended and presented papers with very opposing views. At the end of the convention, the following resolution was adopted with few dissents.

> The congress—
> Considering that the simultaneous use of speech and signs has the disadvantage of injuring speech, lip-reading, and the precision of ideas—
> Declares
> That the pure oral method ought to be preferred (Bender 1981).

Oralism had won in Europe and, subsequently, in the United States. Schools switched from a manual approach to a "pure oral approach" with a few notable exceptions. Gallaudet did succeed in maintaining and fostering the combined methods in several schools and at Columbia College. In a poignantly written article published in 1899, Gallaudet defended his position on the value of sign, saying he felt that "In American and European schools where signs were used with moderation and good judgment . . . the best 'all-around' development of the pupils is secured" (Gallaudet 1997). This position was to receive considerable support nearly seventy years later. Thus, Gallaudet began his career deploring the overuse of signs and finished his career deploring the overuse of oralism. Because of the latter stand, he made a huge contribution to the education of the deaf by emphasizing moderate use of sign.

Because oralism was in accord with the predominant cultural imperatives, it was bound to become the dominant educational method. America, at the turn of the century, was a country of immigrants attempting to assimilate, and the cultural imperative was that everybody should look and act like an "American." Oralism with its emphasis on making deaf children "normal" was closer to the cultural values of the day than manualism and, therefore, prevailed. Moores (1996) very accurately, I think, commented that the battle between Bell and Gallaudet set back education of the deaf because it focused on method rather than pedagogy. It divided educators into warring camps that exist to the present day.

The next 50 years of education of the deaf were essentially what Moores (1996) refers to as the Dark Ages, in which education was in the hands of a few dedicated but inbred educators. On the surface it was placid. The methodology wars had subsided with the deaths of both Gallaudet and Bell. Most deaf children were educated in residential schools using oral techniques by minimally trained teachers. One needed little training to become a teacher of the deaf. It was essentially an apprenticeship system. A 1930s survey of teachers of pre-school deaf children, for example, found that "the majority were under forty, had the usual four years of high school and at least one year of normal school study. . . . Three fifths had not been to college, even fewer to a university. Very few held degrees" (Miller 1997). One became a teacher by in-service training at a school for the deaf. At the time, there were few pre-service training programs at universities. The majority of teachers in schools were either teachers of normally hearing children pressed into service, or poorly educated young women who received their training on the job. This meant that teachers of the deaf did not receive a broad-based education that would enable them to examine different educational philosophies. Instead, they were indoctrinated into the particular educational philosophy or methodology of the school where they worked. They became acolytes or foot soldiers in the methodology war. It is no wonder there was little progress.

However, during the first half of the twentieth century, several notable advances did occur that laid the ground work for the present. Max Goldstein, an otologist in St. Louis, was responsible for bringing a scientific attitude to the education of the deaf by introducing research and technology to the classroom. In 1914, he established the Central Institute for the Deaf (C.I.D.) in St. Louis. The school was private, oral, and had both residential and day students. What set this school apart from others was its close affiliation with Washington University and its heavy emphasis on both clinical and fundamental research into hearing disorders (Bender 1981). Goldstein's landmark book, *The Acoustic Method*, published in 1939, described the use of technology and laboratory science in deaf pedagogy. The Central Institute for the Deaf, in conjunction with Clarke School, was the first to introduce electronic amplification into the classroom. Prior to that, Goldstein had urged the use of a simple hearing tube to stimulate the residual hearing of children. With the advent of the audiometer in 1926, it was possible to demonstrate considerable residual hearing in some children previously identified as deaf and with the development of the vacuum tube hearing aid, which could be worn individually, teachers could be trained to make use of students' hearing in their classrooms. Goldstein was a tireless advocate of the use of amplification to stimulate children's residual hearing. In his book, he noted how hard it was to persuade teachers who emphasized visual training, required by oralism, to include audition training as well. He laid the groundword for the establishment of auralism as the modern means of educating deaf children.

To capitalize on the use of residual hearing, there needed to be a new professional. The audiologist arrived on the scene shortly after the second World War when it was recognized that many of the returning veterans had sustained hearing losses. The combination of otology and speech pathology services at Deshon Army Hospital gave birth to the profession of audiology in the presence of Dr. Raymond Carhart (Ross 1997). Audiology was at first devoted to adult rehabilitation, but then moved to testing and prescription of amplification for children (Ross 1992). Now there was a professional who was concerned with the detection of hearing loss and the use of residual hearing in the habilitation of deaf children.

One other development of note in the first half of this century needs to be recognized—that of pre-school education. Enrollment in the American School for the Deaf began at age ten. With the advent of oralism, and at Bell's insistence, oral schools enrolled children at age five. In 1912, the Ewings began the first pre-school in England (Bender 1981). It is hard to pinpoint who began early childhood education in the United States. There was a nursery as part of C.I. D., and in New York, Mildred Groht, the principal at the Lexington School for the Deaf, was instrumental in promoting early childhood education. Louise Tracy, parent of a deaf child, should get credit for linking pre-school education with parent education. Through her efforts, a clinic, started in 1948, provided an on-site nursery program and a correspondence course for parents (Tracy 1960).

It is notable that significant advances in education of the deaf have come about because of the efforts of parents. Cogswell helped to found the American School that brought manualism; Hubbard was instrumental in developing oral schools; and the Tracys helped bring about the importance of parent education. Without the energy and commitment of these parents, deaf children in the United States would be much worse off than they are today.

In the second half of this century, otologists, audiologists, scientists, and parents, together, prepared to assault the insularity of educators of the deaf. Oralism was favored at the turn of the century because it fit the prevailing cultural imperative of assimilation. In the 1960s America underwent a cultural revolution that was based on race, but actually was a battle for respect of cultural diversity. There was a general mistrust of authority and a push for accountability. It now became respectable (even desirable) to be different. Signing was reintroduced into mainstreamed education of the deaf.

The impetus for change arose from the Babbidge report (1965), a landmark study commissioned by the Government to examine the status of education of the deaf, which indicted educators of the deaf. Babbidge, who was chairman of the commission and president of the University of Connecticut, had no prior knowledge of deafness when he undertook the survey. Looking at education of the deaf with an unprejudiced eye while documenting the results of several studies that indicated deaf graduates were notoriously underachieving, he concluded that educators of the deaf should not be proud of their accomplishments. The vast majority of deaf graduates were working in blue collar jobs with minimal academic and oral English skills. Over 90% of deaf people were married to other deaf people. (This, despite Bell's desire and expectations to the contrary.) Clearly, the oralist's desire to "normalize" deaf people was an abject failure.

Another study which was, I think, the final nail in the oral coffin was research conducted by Stuckless and Birch in 1966. They tested 38 matched pairs of deaf children with a mean age of 18 years. In one group were deaf children of deaf parents; in the other were deaf children of hearing parents. The children were matched as to sex, hearing loss, mental ability, educational attributes, and socioeconomic levels of parents. The variable to be tested was how exposure to early manual communication, as experienced by the deaf children of deaf parents, influenced their linguistic development compared to the language of deaf children of hearing parents who had no exposure to sign. All of the children were attending a school for the deaf at the time of the study. The authors found that both groups had comparable speech intelligibility, but that in the areas of speech reading and reading and writing English, the children who were exposed to early manual communication were superior to the control group (Stuckless and Birch 1966). Subsequent studies by Meadow (1968) and Vernon and Koh (1971) supported the findings that early manual communication seemed to facilitate the acquisition of written English and did not detract from speech intelligibility, despite the view of the oralists that the introduction of signing would detract from the learning of English.

The publication of the book *They Grow in Silence* by Mindel and Vernon in 1971 was a powerful impetus to changing oral education, also. The authors, a psychiatrist (Mindel) and a psychologist (Vernon), documented the emotional effects of failed oralism, which, in turn, led to social and emotional failure. They proposed that deaf children be educated using "total communication," a method in which all modalities are used, including a signed English system. The monolithic oral education structure crumbled very quickly under the combined assaults of manually oriented educators and auditorily minded audiologists.

At present, I can identify five distinct areas of thought regarding educating deaf children. Traditional oralism split into: (1) the auralists who believe in a unisensory approach, (2) the auditory/ oralists who believe in a combined oral/aural approach, (3) total communication which adds a manually coded English system to traditional oralism, (4) the bilingual/bicultural (bi-bi) approach which believes that English should be taught as a second language with American Sign Language as the primary language, and (5) cued speech which attempts to bridge the gap between oral and manual schools by using hand signals that provide phonetic information. One can conceive of these approaches as being on a continuum with, in some cases, not very firm boundaries.

Auralism (Referred to often as Auditory/Verbal in the literature)

Auralism is a unisensory approach that is a natural outgrowth of the work of Goldstein and the development of audiology. It was developed in the United States by Pollack (1993) and Ling (1993). The approach is predicated on the assumption that most deaf children have some residual hearing that can be reached through the use of amplification. Pollock, who called her approach "acoupedics," believed in the necessity of teaching children to listen, something that has to be taught to a hearing impaired child. In order for a deaf child to learn to listen, the visible must be diminished. Emphasis is always on what the child can do auditorily, and Pollock, who trained as a speech pathologist, disliked the term "deaf." She referred to her clients as "limited hearing infants" (1970). Ling (1993), an equally strong proponent of auralism, like Pollock, found ". . . that children do not develop optimal auditory and auditory visual skills unless the use of audition is first developed in the absence of visual cues." In this approach, there is no time set aside for auditory training—it is auditory all the time. Extremely rigid practitioners cover their faces; the more moderate sit alongside or behind the children, ensuring that the children cannot easily see their faces. This approach mandates early detection, fitting with appropriate amplification that is consistently applied, and heavy emphasis on parent involvement. Children, with parents in tow, are usually seen on an individual basis, with direction firmly toward educational mainstreaming and away from schools and programs for deaf children. This approach is most extreme in its attempts to normalize deaf children.

Auditory/Oral

The auditory/oral approach is not as extreme in its auditory demands as auralism. Children are educated, at least for a while, with other deaf students. Therapists and teachers allow, and in some cases, encourage deaf children to look at their faces. It is the modern equivalent of 19th century oralism, with a heavy use of amplification—either the children's individual hearing aids or FM systems. Children are educated within a school or program with other deaf children with a strong emphasis on "auditory training" and lipreading. Emphasis, as with auralism, is on normalizing deaf children and integrating them as soon as possible into mainstreamed education. With auralism, the use of signs and, sometimes, even gestures is discouraged. Both Clarke School and C.I.D. are good examples of this approach.

Total Communication (TC)

Total communication is a term coined by Vernon and Mindel in 1971 and, in many ways, is a rediscovering of the "combined or "simultaneous method" advocated by Edward Miner Gallaudet at the turn of the century. Disillusioned oralists turned to this approach in the late sixties. Because American Sign Language, with its unique syntax and grammar, could not be used readily with English speech (they are two different language systems), they set about modifying ASL to conform to English word order and morphology. Unfortunately, several teams of educators, not communicating with each other, came up with different schemes so that we have three different manually coded English systems: seeing essential English, signing exact English, and signed English. These systems were created primarily for the classroom and were not intended for the deaf community (Stewart 1993). Total communication (TC) seemed to satisfy a perceived need to give the deaf child everything in communication. There is an emphasis on amplification, lip-reading, speech, and a manually coded English system. Schools for the deaf rapidly abandoned oralism and enthusiastically adopted total communication. With relatively few exceptions, most schools for the deaf used TC during the seventies and eighties. A survey of schools in 1979 indicated that nearly two-thirds of all schools used some form of manual communication (Jordan et al.1979).

Bi Lingual/Bi Cultural (Bi-Bi)

The bilingual/bicultural approach is an approach nurtured and maintained at Gallaudet University by faculty and students. This method maintains that deafness is a cultural difference and that deaf people need to be respected and treated as any other cultural minority. Proponents deplore the medical model proposed by the oralists who see deafness as a disorder that needs to be fixed. Proponents also deplore the use of any manually coded English system. American Sign Language (ASL) is considered the natural language of the deaf. Linguistic analysis of ASL indicates that it meets the requirements of a language system (Wilbur 1976), giving educational credence to the movement. The curricular justification and recommendation were spelled out in a position paper by Johnson, Liddell, and Erting (1989). In this working paper, they propose the following:

1. The first language of Deaf children should be a natural sign language (ASL).

2. The acquisition of ASL should begin as early as possible, and the best models for natural sign language acquisition and the development of a

social identity are deaf signers who use the language proficiently. Therefore, they recommend that hearing parents should have extensive contact with adult signers who are brought into the home.

3. Sign language and spoken English are not the same language and must be kept separate. Sign Language is the primary language of instruction and is used to teach English. In short, English is learned as a second language.

4. Speech and the use of amplification, while important, are not to be emphasized in the early instruction of students.

Although the linguists and educators provided the intellectual basis for the bilingual/bicultural approach, an emotional spark was needed to ignite the smoldering fire. In 1988, the fight over the presidency of Gallaudet University provided such a spark. An insensitive board of trustees, dominated by hearing people, had nominated a hearing woman to be the next president of the institution. All previous presidents had also been hearing, but such was the tenor of the times, with disability groups demanding equal access, that there was an open rebellion. The students went on strike and deaf people from all over the United States came to the campus to demonstrate. They forced the resignation of the nominee which led the way to the appointment of the first deaf president. This was a watershed event for the deaf community.

The bilingual/bicultural movement has also achieved educational legitimacy. There has been no recent survey of schools for the deaf in the United States to indicate how many are now using this approach. Of the four schools for the deaf in Massachusetts, two are now using a bi-bi approach; one is using an auditory/oral approach; and the other is using total communication. I suspect the proportion is probably representative of the educational methods currently employed in the United States, with many schools that previously used total communication switching to a bilingual/bicultural model of education.

Cued Speech

Cued speech was developed by R. Orin Cornett in the sixties (Cornett 1967) when he was vice- president of long-range planning at Gallaudet University. Cued speech is a visual system of communication that makes use of eight hand shapes and four locations around the mouth to provide phonetic information to the receiver. It reduces the ambiguity in spoken English by clearly demarcating the homophonous consonants and making visible the visually obscure consonants. It is a manual transliteration of spoken language that makes lip-reading possible, and, as such, is the closest educational method to Bell's written system for visible speech. Cornett has claimed that since there are only 32 different cues, it can be taught and learned in a weekend, using videotapes. (I have tried this and failed miserably; but then again, I have had three beginning sign language courses and I failed those too. I may be hopeless.)

Nichols and Ling (1982), using a syllable and speech recognition measure, tested 18 deaf children who had been using cued speech for at least four years. They found speech reception of over 95% when they tested children with lip-reading and cues. They concluded that "cued speech provides a very effective supplement to restricted audition." Osberger (1997) found that children who used cued speech did as well, after implants, as children who were orally trained. One can infer from the study that cued speech does not interfere with the development of audition.

Cued speech has not been very popular in education of the deaf. The last survey of schools indicated that less than 1% were using it (Jordan et al. 1979). This becomes a self-reinforcing paradigm—early intervention programs do not use cued speech because the schools do not use it because children entering the program have not been exposed to it. Ardent auralists do not like it because it fosters a visual orientation, and ardent manualists do not like it because it is English based. My own view is that this system has much merit; we have had a few children in our nursery using cued speech successfully and it deserves a wider use.

Research is supposed to illuminate, enlighten, and point us in the right direction. The research in deafness, especially when it involves methodology, does neither; it only serves to confuse the issues. Moores (1992) has commented ". . . at the best, results of research may suggest trends and alterations but we should not delude ourselves into thinking that they will sway the opinion of fanatics. Under optimum circumstances, what happens is that, as results accumulate, consensus may be reached on a topic or issue and opinions may shift, but there never will be any final answers" (p. 77).

The research is ambiguous: for example, the landmark study by Stuckless and Birch (1966), which seemed to support the value of early signing on the linguistic development of deaf children, and backed by the studies of Meadow (1967) and Vernon and Koh (1971), are deeply flawed because the families are not at all equivalent. Deaf parents of a deaf child respond very differently from hearing parents to their child's deafness. (I have had deaf parents say to me that they were happy to have a deaf child, that they would not know how to raise a hearing child.) Consequently, the family atmosphere in all respects is very different. The parents are also very fluent signers, which is unlikely to be the case for hearing parents who have to learn sign language from scratch. In order to examine the effects of early signing on English language learning, we need to have children of hearing parents who use signs fluently versus children of hearing parents who did not use signs, or, conversely, deaf parents of deaf children who did not sign. It was nearly impossible to find such children in the 1960s because almost all programs were oral, and there were few hearing parents who knew or used signs. Parasnis (1983) compared deaf college students of deaf parents who were native ASL signers with deaf students of hearing parents who learned sign after the age of six. She used tests of cognitive skills and English language presented through spoken, written, and sign modes. She found no difference in the cognitive and communication performance of both groups. The delayed sign language group performed significantly better than the ASL group on tests of speech perception and speech intelligibility. So it seems that any positive effect that early exposure to signs may impart is washed out by the time a child enters college. In a similar vein, one can find almost an equal number of studies supporting oral education's superiority as those supporting the use of signs; and Schlessinger (1986), in a careful review of methodology studies, concluded that ". . . overall, however, total communication, with its myriad of definitions and as presently carried out, has not had the hoped-for effects in large scale studies; . . ." (p. 105).

In order to test definitely whether or not a given method is better than another, we need to randomly assign large groups of deaf children to different programs matched for quality of instruction. This is not happening, and I do not know if it ever could happen. Then there are all the confounding variables. Audiologists, who function as gatekeepers in recommending programs to parents, usually have some built-in biases. Downs, a pediatric audiologist, developed the deafness management scale (D.M>Q) to help audiologists make decisions regarding educational placement (Northern and Downs 1974). The scale uses hearing loss, intellectual functioning, socioeconomic status, family support, and central nervous system intactness as scale items. Children with a high score (80+) are to be referred to aural/oral programs, while those with scores less than 80 are to attend a total communication program. This means that children with less hearing, less intellect, more central problems, less home support, or those from lower socio-economic homes were assigned to total communication programs. If this is the case, then how is one to do meaningful research into methodology? Investigators try to equate children when they do their research, but the damage is already done. The total communication children are often placed in learning environments that already have low expectations with populations of children who have multiple problems; whereas auditory/oral children are placed among benign populations. The research, then, is not helpful in enabling us to come to any decision regarding methodology. Carney and Moeller (1998) reviewed the efficacy of treatment strategies for deaf children and concluded that the research to date has ". . . been more descriptive than prognostic as to choice of modality. In short, we do not know which children do well in which educational methodology."

If there is any agreement in education of the deaf, and there is not much, it is that education has not been successful. By almost all measures, graduates of schools for the deaf are educational failures. Quigley and Paul (1986) reviewed the studies on educational attainment and concluded ". . . no general educational improvement has been reported . . . nor has any occurred since the studies of Pintner nearly 70 years ago" (p. 81). This lack of progress in educational attainments has occurred despite the shifts in methodology and the advent of technology that have occurred. We have gone to oralism from a manual approach to a combined total communication and, now, to bilingual/bicultural education. The argument of the culturally deaf has been that they cannot do any worse than the other communicative methodologies, which have been in the hands of hearing people (Johnson et al. 1989). To be sure, Quigley and Paul (1986) note in their review, that select students in the superior oral programs do achieve fairly high academic skills, particularly with respect to language and reading. They also note that many of the superior achieving children leave schools for the deaf to become mainstreamed students, and that many of the high achieving deaf children are, therefore, lost to investigators. Moog and Geers (1989), for example, found that many of the mainstreamed orally trained children whom they tested were achieving at grade level, although the aggregate score was still below that of the normally hearing children in English and mathematics. Similar results were found by Schick and Moeller (1992) who tested 13 profoundly deaf mainstreamed children using a manually coded English system (total communication). They found that the deaf students had expressive English skills comparable to the hearing control subjects for some features of English, but showed deficits in some of their morphological skills. Flexer et al. (1993) examined vocabulary skills of 24 orally trained college students who were mainstreamed for most of their education, and found that some of the students (approximately one-fourth) performed as well as their hearing peers (three-fourths did not).

It appears that the results of educating deaf children may be a bit better than the depressing numbers reported in the literature. The more adept students tend to be mainstreamed, and at least some of them are equivalent to their hearing peers in terms of their educational attainments. The overall results, however, are still lower than educators and the deaf community would like. There are still large numbers of deaf children who are demonstrating considerable lags in academic achievement.

My own view is that educators have been fighting the wrong war—the issue is not methodology, but rather pedagogy, under-utilization of technology, and, most importantly, under-utilization of parents. Almost all methods will work considerably better, yielding a higher achieving deaf child, if the teaching is good, if the parents are incorporated into the educational picture, and if technology is utilized fully.

Ross (1992), in his careful review on the use of amplification in educating deaf children notes:

> All such schools possessed classroom amplification systems and most of the children owned hearing aids, but the presence of these devices rarely guaranteed that they were being employed properly. The attempts to stimulate residual hearing that took place in schools before and after World War II seldom seemed to take root and get translated into an in-

formed, enthusiastic, and long-term commitment. In the hundreds of classrooms and schools that I visited over the years, even a superficial examination revealed that audition was rarely used effectively in most of them (p. 21).

This echoes Goldstein's complaint in 1939 that audition was not being utilized in schools for the deaf; and it is doubtful that things have gotten any better. A recent report from the Center for Demographic Studies indicated that 38% of children in schools for the deaf were not wearing hearing aids.

Parents, too, have been systematically excluded from educational programs. Bodner-Johnson (1986), in her review of parental involvement in schools, noted

> . . . parent involvement in school practices in the majority of educational programs for the deaf, as with the rest of regular and special education, are still school initiated. School based activities and school-to-home communication, although worthwhile, represent an imbalance in the partnership family support model . . . . None of these activities depend on or enlist parent general knowledge or involvement (p. 234).

To my way of thinking, parents are the key to the successful education of the child.

In a significant, longitudinal study, Schlessinger (1992), followed forty families, each with a deaf child. She found that the best predictors of literacy for a deaf child were to be found in the linguistic interaction between mother and child which she called this elusive "X factor." It was more important than social class, parental hearing status, the child's hearing status, or IQ. What she found was that school achievement was related to ". . . the clarity and balance in the mother-child verbal interactions, high expectations for children's achievement and maturity, a positive affective relationship, and parental attributes of competence to their children" (p. 39). She comments that ". . . these attributes are found in families that possess a feeling of power and control over their lives regardless of their SES, educational level age or other variables." This statement is much in accord with my own experiences of working with parents of newly diagnosed deaf children. The significant variable is maternal self-esteem. Parents who have good self-esteem will teach language appropriately to their child and will pick out for themselves, over time, the best strategy for communicating with their child. They will solve the methodology issue for themselves.

I think the technological revolution we are currently experiencing in terms of hearing aids and implants will tip the balance in favor of the auralists. My own view is that the bilingual/bicultural movement has peaked and will experience a gradual decline to become marginal again. They are fighting yesterday's wars, and any group that does not anticipate change is usually overwhelmed by it. They are educating deaf children for a world that may not exist twenty years from now. As likely as not, schools for the deaf are going to become mainly repositories for the disadvantaged child, for the multiply handicapped child, and for the deaf child of deaf parents.

The Deaf community is under assault, ironically, because of their very success in removing barriers to communication. The biggest threat to a minority group, outside of genocide, is assimilation; mild to moderate forms of discrimination help maintain the unity of the group. As soon as barriers fall, minority groups become part of the majority and their identity and cohesion are lost. Such is beginning to happen now to the deaf community. The passage of the Americans with Disabilities Act has assured deaf people communicative access to all facets of hearing society. The passage of PL 94-142 mandates educating deaf children in the least restrictive environment, which for many has meant mainstreaming. The changes in educational placement since the passage of that law has been startling. The percentage of deaf children educated in residential schools for the deaf has been dropping from 42% in 1975 to 22% in 1992. In 1992 only 30% of deaf children were educated in schools for the deaf (Johnson and Cohen 1994). This number, I suspect, is lower now as mainstreaming gathers momentum. This is in accord with our current cultural mandate of inclusion and multiculturalism in which we celebrate differences. The dominant cultural theme in the United States has always been towards inclusion, even if we do not, necessarily, do a good job of it. The schools for the deaf have been the major vehicles for acculturating deaf children of hearing parents. With the schools' decline, fewer children of hearing parents will be exposed to deaf culture.

Technology is also making inroads into the cohesiveness of the deaf community. Previously, communication among members of the community was so difficult that, in order to meet and socialize, members had to convene at a deaf club. Now, like their hearing counterparts, they can stay home, watch TV or a movie with closed captioning, and communicate with anyone via TTY, fax, or e-mail. The deaf club, which has been in decline as noted by Lane et al. (1996), was the major social and acculturating vehicle for deaf adults, as was the residential school.

Whether bi/bi methodology can work as an educational philosophy is questionable. It has been launched without any research support or justification, and seems more an angry reaction by members of the deaf community to the intrusion of hearing professionals. Arguments justifying its use have come from teaching English as a second language to foreign speaking children. Fluency in one language is necessary before a second language can be learned (Barnum 1984). To transfer the experience with foreign speaking children to deaf education is questionable at best. Foreign speaking children learned their primary language from competent and native speaking role models, as do deaf children of deaf parents. Can bi/bi work when hearing parents are being asked to learn a new language and then teach this to their child? We know that children have to be immersed in a language in order to learn it. Swisher and Thompson (1985) reported that hearing mothers who had learned simultaneous communication by using manually coded English only signed 40% of their utterances. With such limited signing, can deaf children learning the language get sufficient reinforcement? I seriously doubt it. Importing deaf role models into the family, as suggested by Johnson et al. (1989) is, I think, a doubtful strategy at best, and to try to bypass the parents will not work. The last person a parent of a newly diagnosed deaf child wants to see is a deaf adult who is not speaking. (See survey results in next chapter.) In the early stages of parents' psychological adjustment, they are usually resistant, hoping that their child will be "super deaf," meaning much like the hearing child they were supposed to have, and they are not ready to meet a non-vocal deaf adult.

Teaching ASL as the primary language seems to me to be rediscovering the wheel. There is very little difference between the current bi/bi approach and that advocated by Gallaudet and Laurent Clerc in the 1820s at the American School. There is no evidence that 19th century deaf children achieved English literacy any better than orally trained deaf children of the 20th century. By inference, we have Edward Miner Gallaudet's complaint that there was too much sign and not enough oral English exposure because the 19th century deaf child was not learning English—I don't think the 20th century child is learning it either. To my way of thinking, the bi/bi experiment in education has been launched without any research justification as an angry, emotional response by many badly treated orally educated deaf adults. The losers, again, will be deaf children caught in a diminishing system, ill prepared for competing in the 21st century. I think we will be creating a generation of deaf adults who will be very angry that they were not given a chance to learn to speak, with resultant limited social and vocational choices.

In a similar vein, the auralists, with their promises to normalize deaf children, are sometimes insensitive to children's developmental and social needs. These children often grow up socially isolated, having lost large pieces of their childhood. The measure of success for auralists of all stripes is the child's speech and English language skills. This is, however, too narrow a measure; though quantifiable, it does not tell the whole story. Many highly achieving deaf children have identity crises as they grow older. Despite impressive performances as deaf children, they still do not measure up to hearing peers. They are like Eliza Doolittle in *My Fair Lady*, with good speech and no place to go. In many social situations with hearing peers, they are at a disadvantage. Because they have been denied access to the deaf community, they usually have limited or non-existent signing skills. Consequently, they fit in neither group. In a survey of families who graduated from our nursery program, we found that parents who had gone the aural/oral/ mainstreamed route were most unhappy about their child's social adjustment, many reporting that their child had no friends. Parents who had gone the school for the deaf route with signing were happy about their child's social adjustment, but unhappy about their academic achievements (Luterman 1995). If we are to be truly successful in educating deaf children, we are going to have to have the complete package: An adult with high self-esteem, who is able to move comfortably between and within the deaf and hearing worlds.

At the Emerson nursery, the approach that seems to work best with the children in regards to methodology, is one in which we use a manually coded English system with a heavy emphasis on amplification. Our general philosophy is that the child will teach us how he or she wants to learn. All teaching is regarded as diagnostic; we have no methodological bias. We find that, contrary to the auralists, the judicious use of sign, as proposed by Edward Miner Gallaudet, reduces the frustration between parent and child and does not interfere with the development of auditory mindedness or speech. We find, as the child becomes more verbal, that signing is dropped. For those children who do not develop well auditorily, the signing becomes increasingly important. (Contrary to the bi/bi philosophy, I think it is easier for deaf children to learn ASL after they have English rather than the other way around.)

The entire program is embedded within a philosophy of empowering parents, which we find is the most efficacious way of helping children. (See chapter 3.) No educational method is going to work unless parents freely choose it and take responsibility for it. Parents will find the best solutions for themselves, which may or may not be what an educator would choose. Recently, one family in our nursery decided to put their son with a newly acquired cochlear implant into an ASL based program because they wanted him immersed in sign with access to the culturally deaf community. At the same time, they wanted him to have sufficient oral skills to be able to compete with hearing people. Will this work? I do not know. But it will be interesting to find out. Empowered parents will come up with unique solutions, and, according to the Schlessinger study (1992), provide good language stimulation for their child.

The future in education of the deaf is now. Deaf children will be identified early (many at birth, see next chapter), and fit with superior amplification. Many of those very deaf infants (or not so deaf), who would have been prime candidates for a school for the deaf with access to the culturally deaf community, will now have a cochlear implant and join the world of the hard of hearing. These children are more likely to be enrolled in a public school system. I am not at all sure we are ready for these children. The study of Farrugia and Austin (1980) demonstrated that hearing impaired children, educated in the mainstream, have lower self-esteem than children educated in schools for the deaf. A similar concern was expressed by Johnson and Cohen (1994). Moores (1992) has commented: "Although there always have been some deaf individuals who have developed excellent expressive and receptive oral skills, and who have chosen to integrate fully into hearing society, sometimes at great emotional costs, it is undeniable that assimilation, completely on terms set by the hearing world, does not work" (p. 74). We, the professional community, in conjunction with parents, will need to work out social structures for this new generation of deaf children. Ross (1992) has wisely commented:

> There are no ideal solutions. For our audiologic "successes," we have dealt with the condition and reduced its impact considerably. The auditory/verbal accomplishments of some of these children are amazing, but the hearing loss still remains as an impediment to communication in many ordinary situations. Some of these children are strong, self-confident individuals who know and accept the real limitations of their hearing loss and rise above them. Others, regardless of their linguistic accomplishments, eventually come to an identity crisis which they must painfully resolve. . . . Choices will have to be made but this is a distinguishing characteristic of human beings; life would be much easier if our range of choices were more limited—but it would also be a life less uniquely human. (p. 4)

I see the beginnings of organizational support with the establishment of implant clubs, but I do not see an equivalent concern for the hard of hearing child or the aurally trained deaf child. Despite all of our technological advances, we are not curing their deafness; we are providing the deaf child with communication access. They will need considerable institutional and social support in order to truly succeed. We currently have at hand all the necessary tools to eliminate the negative educational consequences of deafness. The question is whether or not we will use these tools intelligently to produce an adult who is comfortable with his or her deafness, and able to access both hearing and deaf "worlds."

CHAPTER 2

Early Detection

It is almost axiomatic in the field of education of the deaf that early detection and early intervention will yield a better functioning hearing impaired child. In general, there is research support for this notion. Greenstein (1975) studied 30 deaf children enrolled in programs before the age of two and followed them until they were past the age of three. She found that children who were in the program before the age of 16 months showed greater language competency than their deaf peers who were enrolled after 16 months. Mankowitz and Larson (1990) studied 646 children in special education programs in Montgomery County, Maryland and found that children who were enrolled in these programs at earlier ages benefited more than those children who started later.

Watkins (1987), reporting on a home intervention program involving nearly 21,000 children, found that hearing impaired children who received home-based early intervention services performed significantly better in several language and educational areas than children who did not receive such services. The one dissenting study by Musselman et al. (1988), using regression equations, looked at children enrolled in early intervention programs and found that spoken and receptive language outcomes were not related to ages of intervention. Yoshinaga-Itano (1997), however, recently reported preliminary data indicating that children whose hearing losses were identified before 6 months of age showed significantly higher expressive language quotients than children identified after 6 months old.

The difficulty shared by these researchers is trying to equate families and children. Families that identify their children very early and participate in early intervention programs are likely to be different from those families that do not, and any retrospective study needs to account for this difference. I think the only way to resolve this issue would be to have a large-scale study in which early identified children were randomly assigned to either early intervention programs or no therapy. This study cannot be done for ethical reasons, and so we are left with our intuitions and some less than perfect research. Carney and Moeller (1998), in their comprehensive review of the treatment efficacy of early intervention concluded:

> Early identification of hearing loss and enrollment in intervention is the first line of defense in reducing the consequences of hearing loss. The most recent results from early intervention programs have been found to be effective in reducing the extent of delay a child experiences and in easing familial stress reactions. Thus, early intervention may be considered effective, based on current research (p. 578).

This seems to me to be a fair assessment of the current thinking regarding early intervention. So, armed with their intuitions and research support, audiologists in general have been mounting a campaign to screen the hearing of all newborns, a vital element in early intervention programs.

The reasonable assumption is that if a child is identified early and habilitation instituted, the educational outcome will be improved. Newborn screening for hearing impairment is not a new idea. I can remember in the 1960s participating in a study with trained volunteers with pads in their hands standing around a crib of a newborn infant to judge whether the infant responded to sounds produced by an array of instruments. We used some low-pitched stimuli generated by horns or a male voice and high pitched sounds using bells. The judgments were then tabulated to see if the infant "heard," or more accurately, responded. Unfortunately, despite our best efforts, the judgments were never sufficiently reliable for us to feel we had a procedure that would work. It was also difficult to coordinate the volunteers' schedules with the arrival of the newborns.

We then graduated to the crib-o-grams in which infants were placed on mats that registered any movements they might make in response to sound stimuli without benefit of judges. This, too, was found to be unreliable since many normally hearing newborns slept soundly and would not react to the sounds, thus, giving an enormous number of false positives and causing this test also to be abandoned (Smith et al. 1985).

Over the past thirty years, several different procedures for screening newborns, including cardiac response, respiration audiometry, or alteration of sucking and startle responses have been used, investigated, and found wanting. It was not until the advent of auditory brainstem response (ABR) testing, which measures the evoked electrophysiological response to auditory stimuli at the brainstem, that sufficiently reliable responses could be obtained without the voluntary cooperation of the child, making the testing of newborns feasible. Electrodes placed on the child's skull record brainstem responses to a variety of auditory stimuli. This, however, is a rather costly procedure, requiring a trained audiologist to administer and interpret the data. Consequently, it could not be used as a universal screening tool, and, instead, has been used in conjunction with a "high risk register." With this program, only at-risk infants who qualify are given ABR tests. The criteria for inclusion in the register were determined by a Joint Committee of the American Academy of Otolaryngology, the American Academy of Pediatrics, and the American Speech and Hearing Association (ASHA, Joint Committee 1991).

Risk Factors for Neonates

1. Family history of congenital or delayed-onset childhood sensorineural hearing loss.

2. Congenital infection known or associated with sensorineural hearing loss: cytomegalovirus, rubella, herpes, toxoplasmosis, syphilis.

3. Craniofacial anomalies, including abnormalities of the pinna and ear canal, low hairline, and absent philtrum.

4. Birth weight less than 1500 grams (3.3 pounds).

5. Hyperbilirubinemia—at levels exceeding indications for exchange transfusion.

6. Ototoxic medications, including, but not limited to, the aminoglycosides, (e. g., gentamycin, kanamycin, streptomycin) used for more than five days and certain diuretics used in combination with these days.

7. Bacterial meningitis.

8. Severe depression at birth, which may include infants with apgar scores of 0-3 at five minutes,

those who fail to initiate spontaneous respiration by ten minutes, or those with hypotonia persisting to two hours of age.

9. Prolonged mechanical ventilation for a duration equal to or greater than ten days.

10. Stigmata or other findings associated with a syndrome known to include sensorineural hearing loss.

This procedure seems to pick up about half of newborns with hearing loss because some hearing impaired newborns with no known risks do not meet these criteria (Elssman et al. 1987; Mauk et al. 1991). I suspect the number of children who are not identified is also due to an inadequate implementation of the register because physicians and hospital personnel do not always inform parents about it, or they, themselves, are not aware of the indications for testing. Over the years, we have had several families in the nursery who met the criteria for testing, but were not informed of their eligibility despite the fact that Massachusetts has had a high-risk register for over ten years. Adequate implementation of a high-risk register requires continuous inservice training of hospital personnel to remind them of the test criteria regarding neonates.

Recently, the ABR has been automated and another test—Evoked Otoacoustic Emission (EOAE)—has been developed. Both of these procedures can be rapidly administered by trained volunteers or technicians, thus making universal screenings for hearing impairment economically feasible.

In 1993, the National Institutes of Health (NIH) convened a consensus development conference to examine the feasibility of universal screening for newborns. The consensus reached by the panel was that it is now feasible and desirable to screen all newborns. They recommended a two-stage protocol using evoked otoacoustic emissions testing for all infants followed by auditory brainstem testing for those infants who fail the EOAE testing. The panel report concluded with the following caveat: "Clearly, universal screening will increase the number of infants identified with hearing impairment. This will necessitate adequate diagnostic follow-up and treatment facilities. Comprehensive intervention and management programs must be an integral part of a universal screening program" (National Institute of Health 1993).

As a result of the NIH recommendation (and even prior to it), several states, notably Rhode Island, Colorado, and Hawaii had instituted universal screening of newborns, and many hospitals throughout the country were screening for hearing loss without a state mandate. Several articles appeared extolling and supporting the value of early detection and screening (Hermann 1994; Northern and Hayes 1994; Mauk and White 1995; Downs 1995; Robinette and White 1997).

Shortly after the publication of the NIH report, Bess and Paradise (1994) took issue with the conclusions of the NIH panel; they did not feel that universal newborn screening was justified at that time because of: (1) the high number of false positives that would result; (2) the increased cost for the limited yield, and (3) the lack of available trained personnel for follow-up and treatment. They concluded their paper with the following statement:

> We, too, believe that early identification is important; however, the precipitous launching of mass screening could well work to deter the eventual development of an effective early

identification program. In the meantime, to identify infants at risk for hearing impairment, continued reliance on the high risk register as recommended by the Joint Committee on Infant Hearing but in combination with an automated rather than conventional ABR screen, seems to be a more practical, cost effective approach. (p. 334)

The publication of this paper led to several articles and editorials refuting their arguments.

Northern and Hayes (1994) felt that Bess and Paradise's points were not valid and that "We must not be deterred by critical commentaries which undermine and delay identification of children with hearing loss." They concluded their review of the screening literature with the following:

1. Sensorineural hearing impairment in infants and young children is a serious condition which results in life-long disability.

2. Continued dependence on the 1990 high-risk registry approach to screening infants will identify less than fifty percent of infants with significant hearing loss.

3. Valid techniques, with proven acceptable sensitivity and specificity, are currently available to detect moderate, severe, and profound hearing loss in infants.

4. Early intervention is essential for facilitating speech, language, and cognitive skills, as well as social-emotional development, and academic achievement. (p. 3)

White and Maxon (1995), using data obtained from the universal screening program in Rhode Island that uses a two-stage protocol similar to that recommended by the NIH panel, concluded that universal screening of hearing was justifiable and cost-effective. According to their calculations, hearing loss screening is about one tenth the cost per child identified as being hearing impaired that we currently pay to identify children with hypothyroidism, phenylketononia, or sickle cell anemia. Based on their experience with the Rhode Island program they felt "Universal newborn hearing screening is practical, effective, cost efficient, and safe; such programs should be implemented without further delay" (White and Maxon 1995). They did not, however, publish any data on the number of false positives, that is, those children who fail the initial screen, but on subsequent testing are found to have normal hearing. As we shall see, this is a persistent problem of the testing procedure and of definition, so that it is difficult for the reader to know what criteria for a false positive is being used. In Rhode Island, a false positive is defined as a failure on the second testing, although the child is later found to have normal hearing. The parents are not told that anything is wrong with their child; they are simply asked to return for the second part of the screening. In other states and studies, a false positive is defined as a failure on the first in-hospital screening and a subsequent pass on the second test. Downs (1995), in describing the Colorado experience in which screening used just a one-stage protocol of an automated ABA procedure, found that out of 100 initial failures, 94 passed the follow-up test. Of the six confirmed sensorineural hearing losses, three would have been detected by the high-risk register. Nevertheless, she was still enthusiastic about universal screening for newborns despite the high number of false positives.

Tharpe and Clayton (1997), on the other hand, feel that such a high number of false positives does not justify universal screening. They point out that mis-identified neonates can become "vulnerable children," and even though a second stage screening procedure might eliminate a larger number of false positives, as indicated by the Rhode Island experience (Maxon et al. 1995), it would not matter to the parents; from their perspectives what matters is that they were told that their child may have something seriously wrong with him or her. Once this idea is implanted in parents' minds, it is hard to remove.They also expressed concerns about the ethical considerations regarding informed parental permission and whether or not screening should be voluntary. (In Rhode Island, the parents are informed prior to birth and have the right to refuse at any time.) Legal issues also arise in the failure to perform screening adequately and audiologists would be legally liable for screening failures.

Abdala de Uzcategui and Yoshinaga-Itano (1997), in a survey of parents in Colorado with normal hearing children who failed the first screening procedure (i.e., the false positives), found that 78% were not angry at having to go through the testing procedure a second time. They did not report on the emotions of the remaining 22%, who were less than happy, although, at one hospital, 11% of parents expressed anger and shock that this was happening to them. They also reported that 25% of the initial screening failures at each hospital did not return for further testing, indicating that there are still many holes in the testing and management protocols.

Recently, Mehl and Thompson (1998) reported new data on the Colorado experience of 1996, in which 41,796 children were screened using automated ABR and/or otoacoustic emission testing. Two thousand seven hundred nine failed the initial screen; 1,296 children were reevaluated. Of the 1,296 children reevaluated, 94 were identified with congenital sensorineural hearing loss, and 32 were identified with conductive loss. According to my statistics, this still yields a false positive rate of nearly 91%, that is, nearly nine out of every ten children who failed the initial screen were found to have normal hearing on the reevaluation. Neither Downs nor Mehl and Thompson seem to be concerned about the psychological or economic consequences of such a high false positive rate. I know of no other screening test that yields such a high number.

Similar results are reported in the Hawaii experience (Mason and Hermann 1998). In a five-year study of screening 10,372 newborn infants, there were 415 failures on the initial screen using an automated ABR, or approximately 4% of the test population. Of these 415 children, 15 were found to have a significant bilateral hearing loss requiring amplification. The false positive rate was also in excess of 90%. Thirty-eight children, or nearly 10%, were lost to follow-up.

It is very hard to compare studies, because the authors report their statistics differently and a reader has to wend his way through them. In Rhode Island, which has the oldest established initial two-stage otoacoustic emissions universal screening program, the initial failure referral of 7% of all newborns was reduced to 1% with careful modifications of the testing protocols (Maxon et al. 1995). The study did not give the false positive rate, but even a 1% failure rate would still yield 90% false positives, as the incidence of congenital bilateral sensorineural loss is generally considered to be 1 per 1000 in the well-baby population (Mason and Hermann 1998).

The problem of the high false positive rate is not in the test, which has a sensitivity of 100% and a specificity of 97% (Hermann et al. 1995) for the automated ABR, but in the test protocols. The newborn infant is not a good candidate for testing because of the possible presence of birth debris and amniotic fluid in the canal, and distortions in the external meatus caused by the birth process. All of these can cause temporary conductive hearing loss which clears up spontaneously within the first few weeks, and sometimes hours, after birth.

Maxon et al. (1997) have also demonstrated that the refer rate can be dramatically reduced by good screening training, which includes the handling of the baby as well as technicians' education in test technique. Additionally, if attention is paid to the external ear canal, so that efforts are made to open collapsed canals and clean out debris present, referral rates can be controlled. They note that good test technique with well-fitted probes and the use of appropriate software to filter out low-frequency noise will also reduce referral rates to less than 1%. The referral rates in Colorado, with good techniques, are as low as 2% (Mehl and Thompson 1998), and in Hawaii 4% (Mason and Hermann 1998), both of which would still yield a false positive rate in excess of 90%. The authors of these studies extol the number of identified children and seem to ignore the false positives.

Calculating the actual cost of identifying a child as deaf is also difficult to determine because different investigators use a variety of formulae to calculate cost, including amortization of equipment and projections of numbers of children to be tested. Table I presents data showing a wide range in costs, with Rhode Island being the least expensive at $4,378 per identified child. In part, the Rhode Island figure is low because of the way in which it was calculated, representing only the cost of screening and not the cost of identification, and because of the determined effort made in that state to reduce false positives. The data from Rhode Island, Colorado, and Hawaii are summarized in table I.

The actual costs, however, for each newly identified child should be doubled since 50% of the children would have been identified by using the high-risk register. If we add in the cost of lost work hours for parents whose children were among the false positives and had to be retested unnecessarily, then the expense becomes truly prohibitive.

Is it worth it? It is hard to put a monetary price on the habilitative advantages for a few children. At this point, I agree with Bess and Paradise (1994) that the risk benefit ratio does not seem to justify universal testing. I cannot help but wonder if the energy and expense currently being expended on promoting screening were to be used in vigorously promoting the high-risk register and expanding public and professional education about hearing loss, would we not get comparable results without the enormous current actual and psychological cost of newborn screening. What also gives me pause concerning screening is the fact that not all parents of deaf children would have wanted to know at birth that their child was deaf because it would have interfered with the bonding of their child (Luterman and Kurtzer-White 1998).

Table I   False Positive and Cost Per Identified Child By State

State	False Positive	Cost per Identified Child
Colorado1	94%	$ 9,600.
Hawaii2	93%	$17,750.
Rhode Island3	50-60% Estimated	$ 4,378.

Sources: 1 Mehl and Thompson (1998)
             2 Mason and Hermann (1998)
             3 Maxon et al. (1995)

Despite my concerns, there is clearly a consensus forming that early detection of hearing loss is desirable and feasible, albeit with a high cost. The American Speech-Language-Hearing Association (1997) has recently strongly endorsed federal legislation—(HR2923) The Early Hearing Loss Detection, Diagnosis and Intervention Act—which would provide monetary incentives for states to initiate universal hearing screening programs for newborns. The American Speech-Language-Hearing Association will provide model legislation to those states that wish to set up a universal screening program. With a push from the Federal government and ASHA, universal screening has a momentum of its own and will, I think, become a reality in most states. It behooves us, then, as professionals, to do this well.

The devil, however, is in the details. While the technology is here, the human issues have not been addressed. There are two cogent problems of the screening protocols that need to be looked into, namely, the high number of false positives, as Bess and Paradise predicted, and the low compliance rate of parents returning for the second test.

The false positive rate, as much as 94% in the Colorado and Hawaii studies (Down 1995; Mason and Hermann 1998), cannot be taken lightly. This is much too high, not only because of the follow-up costs to hospitals tracking these initial failures and the additional expense to parents who have to return for additional testing, but also because of the potential stress it places on those compliant families waiting to return for the outpatient rescreening. Once the idea that there might be something wrong with the child is implanted in the family, emotional stress can ensue. This stress is also occurring at a very critical juncture in the infant's life, when he or she must bond with the parents. For the newborn, basic trust is being established (Erikson 1950) and having a worried, upset parent potentially can interfere with the process of establishing trust in the child's first and critical relationship with his or her parents. The false positive, then, is not a benign or neutral event. It has the potential to cause harm.

In a similar vein, the lack of compliance (25% in the Colorado study) has to be of concern. Audiologists can ill afford to lose this population because a relatively high percentage of these children will have an actual loss. Care needs to be taken in how and when parents are informed of their child's failure to pass the initial screening. The "blame" should be put on the test, which, given the high false positive, may be where it belongs; but the dilemma is that the more the test is blamed, the less likely it is that the parents will return. It feeds into the denial mechanism. Why should they return if the test results are most likely to be unreliable? On the other hand, if the results are given in such a way that they alarm the parents, then interference with the parent-child bonding can ensue. The parents may also be scared sufficiently so they do not return. The third possibility is that audiologists expose themselves to litigation. Tharpe and Clayton (1997) have pointed out that it is the audiologist who has the legal liability for causing undue stress.

When parents are told is also an issue that needs to be addressed; as in most things in life, timing is everything. Most programs seem to inform parents in the hospital shortly before discharge. There is never a good time to give parents what may be bad news, but I cannot think of a worse time then shortly after they have given birth. The parents are both emotionally and physically exhausted and are in no position to process cognitive material, especially if it might be negative. There are several programs, in Rhode Island most notably, that wait several weeks before informing parents of the screening results. It would be interesting to compare the compliance rates from various programs in terms of how and when parents are informed. My own guess is that there would be higher compliance rates if there was a gap between testing and informing, which would allow the parents to be more receptive, having recovered from the stress of the birth. It is in such mundane details as these that the success or failure of a screening program rests. Each program will have to conduct ongoing self-evaluations by canvassing parents who have been through the screening process to determine the best way and the best time to inform parents of a child's screening failure. I suspect that the "best" procedure will vary from program to program depending on the population served.

There is almost nothing in the literature indicating what would constitute a good management program, despite the very clear recommendations of the NIH panel that no screening programs be instituted unless a comprehensive intervention and management program is in place. The controversy in the literature has been mainly about whether or not to test, but not about how to manage. Luterman and Kurtzer-White (1998) have surveyed parents of hearing impaired children to determine their needs, following detection of hearing impairment. Seventy-four parents of deaf children completed a five-item questionnaire with the following results:

1. Eighty-three percent of the parents would have wanted to know at birth that their child was deaf. The 17% who preferred a later diagnosis

were concerned with the effect the diagnosis would have on the parent-child bonding process. They preferred a diagnosis at a later time, the majority preferring a time before the child is one year old.

2. Parents preferred the audiologist to be the one to inform them about their child's deafness. There were very few responses (6%) indicating a preference for having a mental health professional inform them.

3. Their biggest needs at the time of diagnosis were contact with other parents, unbiased information, help with their feelings, and getting started with services. Less than 10% of the parents indicated that they wanted to meet deaf adults.

We can begin to discern the shape of a good management program from the responses of the parents. There is clearly support for early detection, although it is not unanimous that this occur at birth. To me, a good compromise is seen in the Rhode Island program where they inform the parents three weeks after testing. This allows parents time to recover from the birth process and enables them to have some time to enjoy having a newborn. There is no evidence in the literature to indicate that the delay of one month in diagnosis will have any negative habilitative consequences for the child, and it might increase the compliance rates. It is absolutely essential, though, that the follow-up evaluation be done shortly after notifying the family. To leave the family hanging in their anxiety would be cruel.

Bess and Paradise (1994), again, were on the mark when they expressed concern about the number of skilled personnel and programs that would be available following a screening program. We can expect a large increase in the number of hearing impaired children entering the early intervention system as a result of newborn screening. We can expect deaf children to stay in the system longer since they would be picked up at birth. As noted by Mehl and Thompson (1998) in the Hawaii experience, screening picks up milder hearing losses, such as children with unilateral losses and mild to moderate losses both conductive and sensorineural that would have been detected much later, were it not for the screening. The question remains whether there are sufficiently trained personnel in place to handle the increased load, especially in light of the fact that ASHA has recently cut back on the number of aural rehabilitation practicum hours required for certification. To notify parents that they now have a hearing impaired child without having a satisfactory management program in place would be cruel. And, presently, I do not see very much energy, thought, or training being given to the management side of the equation.

Counseling issues also need to be addressed. They are formidable. Most testing for suspected hearing loss in young children is parent driven, as parents slowly become aware there might be something wrong with their child's hearing. After much inconsistent behavioral testing, parents usually consult an audiologist. Very often, the audiologist can become an ally by confirming the parents' concerns, and counseling becomes relatively easy. Counseling parents whose children have been identified by a screening program, when they have been unaware of any problem and are physically and emotionally exhausted by the birth process, is going to be formidable. Parents who had children with confirmed hearing loss in the Abdala de Uzcategui and

Yoshinaga-Itano survey (1997) in Colorado, had a ". . . higher level of impatience/frustration with the process and were more sure that a hearing loss existed after the initial screening but before the confirmation. They also expressed more anger (that this was happening to them), depression, and confusion than did those parents whose children did not have a hearing loss."

People often kill the messenger when they do not like the message, and the audiologist is going to be in the direct line of fire, ill prepared for the onslaught. Not only are audiologists going to have to deal with an angry, frustrated parent of a hearing impaired child, they are also going to have to deal with the angry "false positive" parents. A recent survey by Crandell (1997) indicates that only an estimated 18% of graduating audiologists have taken a course in counseling; so we are sending forth audiologists who have almost no exposure to good counseling techniques in their training programs to deal with very difficult, emotionally charged situations. This has all the elements of a disaster.

Parents have a need for unbiased information. This information needs to be spaced over time. In the initial stages of diagnosis, the affect in most parents is so great that they cannot absorb content, especially the complex and controversial information in education of the deaf. They will need to master information regarding the technology of hearing aids and cochlear implants, as well as data concerning methodology. Unfortunately, referral to an educational facility in most states is not productive because most educational programs are methodology driven and "education" for both the child and the parent is usually directed at convincing them of the values of their own particular method. Rarely is a parent exposed to a range of educational options within a program; rarely is a child exposed to diagnostic teaching to determine which way he or she learns best; and rarely is a family helped in the decision about which educational option best suits their needs. Such programs need to be created where they do not currently exist if audiologists are going to promote universal screening of newborns vigorously. Audiologists must take responsibility for the after-care program to ensure that parents receive the unbiased information they need. Programs will also need to provide ample opportunities for parents to have contact with other parents. An ongoing support group is ideal. Lacking that, a mentoring program or an intensive family vacation weekend might be an adequate substitute in rural areas. These programs will be described in more detail in the next chapter.

This, then, is an outline of what I consider to be the essence of a good management program:

1. Continual work on devising a better screening procedure to eliminate or reduce the false positives. In the meantime, an enhanced high risk register with expanded public and professional education.

2. Delay between newborn screening and informing parents, with a very short interval between notification and the second test.

3. Continuous inservice training for audiological personnel to help them learn how to inform and counsel parents.

4. Ongoing programmatic self-evaluation to determine the best procedures for informing parents.

5. Contact with other parents of hearing impaired children either through a formal program offer-

ing a support group or a registry of mentoring, experienced parents.

6. Ongoing diagnostic teaching within a family-centered program for the parent and child without methodology pressure or bias.

CHAPTER 3

Programs

Programming for the newly identified hearing impaired child must be parent and family centered. At this point, the child does not have the problem—the parent does. I have been encouraged by the growing recognition of this basic proposition throughout our profession. The reader is referred to the excellent text *Infants and Toddlers with Hearing Loss* edited by Roush and Matkin. Exemplary programs, all family centered, are described in this text. These are model programs that can be modified and adapted to particular areas of the country.

To fulfill the NIH mandate, three kinds of intervention and management programs can be adapted to use in conjunction with a state-wide screening program or enhanced high-risk register: itinerant, short-term intensive, and center based. These programs are not necessarily mutually exclusive, and can be blended. Exemplary state-wide programs will use all three components.

Itinerant

The itinerant program is not my favorite type in that, administratively, it is very expensive. Someone has to pay for the high-priced therapist's time spent in a car.

This program also puts an enormous responsibility on the visiting teacher, as he or she often has to assume many different roles, including social worker, when entering the home. Not only is the home visitor a communication therapist to the child, but also a support service for the emotional needs of the parents. Especially in rural areas, the therapist is literally on the firing line, as he or she is very often the only professional that a parent has contact with on a regular basis. There is a tendency on the part of parents to develop a dependent relationship on the therapist, which often goes beyond the traditional scope of practice or competency of a speech-language-pathologist/parent trainer. All itinerant programs need to be heavily parent centered because, invariably, there are few contact hours between the professional and the child. There is an inverse relationship between the amount of time available and the degree of family focus; with limited time, there must be maximum family involvement.

An interesting study, however, indicates that professional intervention is not always helpful. Sandow and Clark (1977) studied the effects of a home intervention program on the performance of severely impaired preschool children, mainly those with Down syndrome and severe cerebral palsy. The 32 children were divided into two matched groups as to severity of disorder. In a three-year study, one group of families was visited by a therapist once every two weeks for a two-hour session, while the other group, which lived more distant from the center, was seen once every two months. The children were tested periodically for progress on their cognitive functioning and speech and language development. The findings were rather startling. Initially, the children who were visited more frequently showed more gains in intellectual growth and in speech and language than children who were visited less frequently.

As the study progressed, however, researchers found that the children who were visited less frequently began to show more gains, and, in the third year, the gains increased. Sandow and Clark suggested that the parents of the children who were more frequently visited became more dependent on the therapist than the parents who were less frequently visited, and therefore, did not follow through on the therapy—they waited for the therapist to "fix" the child.

My own view is that itinerant therapists who do not a have strong parent-centered orientation often diminish the parents self-esteem. When the home visitor is child-centered, with only a limited time, the therapist, to ensure success, often gives the lesson to the child with the parent passively observing. These lessons are usually successful because the therapist is competent and the child is usually cooperative. The therapist also brings in toys that the child has not seen. When the parent tries to follow through on what has been so easily demonstrated, he or she fails for a variety of reasons: the child is too familiar with the parent and resents the parent as therapist; the parent is often too emotionally involved to see what the child needs and is conducting "therapy" in an environment, the home, where too many distractions and other pressures interfere with the process; and finally, there is no reason to assume that the parents are competent to give lessons. Why should they be? In programs where professionals consistently demonstrate their competence, the parents' confidence is subtly undermined, fostering parental dependency on the therapist. This is the potential pitfall of the itinerant program, which requires highly skilled, sensitive clinicians who have a strong parent focus. They must see the parent as the recipient of their "therapy" and must build parent self-esteem at every opportunity.

I have worked with groups of itinerant teachers in rural areas; invariably, I find that they are young, and, if older, have been newly hired. I suspect the burnout rate is very high, both from the amount of travel required and from the awesome amount of personal and professional responsibility they are asked to assume on the job. I feel itinerant programs, especially in rural areas, are a necessary and desirable component of a comprehensive management program. They are, however, at best, band-aid treatments, tricking administrators into thinking they have a complete program.

The first step in doing an itinerant program well is the careful selection of the itinerant teacher. He or she needs to be trained and supported carefully from a center-based program. One such program has been described by Brown and Yoshinago-Itano (1994) in Colorado. There, home visitors are selected from a variety of backgrounds, including speech-language pathology, audiology, education of the deaf, and early childhood. In the Washington state program (Thompson 1994), several parent facilitators are mothers of hearing impaired children, who were graduates of the state-wide early intervention program. Thompson found that the mothers were among the best of the parent facilitators because they had instant credibility and could easily gain the trust of parents in the program. The mothers/teachers also tended to be more sensitive to the needs of the parents, more so than untested, recent graduates of training programs. I, too, have found a similar result, and have often hired parents of older deaf children to be nursery teachers or therapists.

I have long felt that experienced parents of deaf children, who receive additional training, are a huge untapped resource to a comprehensive state-wide program in deafness management. They can be used, for example, as mentors/tutors to those marginally adequate families where there is a hearing impaired child. These are families that do not have many resources, either educational or familial, to do an adequate job in management of the hearing impaired child. Older, experienced parents can serve as a support system by "adopting" the family, in addition to the professional support provided by the itinerant or center-based program.

The exemplary itinerant programs also provide ongoing inservice and center based support for the parent facilitators (Thompson 1994; Brown and Yoshinago-Itano 1994). I think this is essential to prevent facilitator burnout and to provide them with a support structure. In the Washington state program, they have more than one facilitator visit a home so that there are at least two different points of view about a family and child. This enables the professionals to compare notes and also limits the development of dependent relationships. Administrators of an itinerant program must constantly maintain vigilance in the training and support of the home visitors. This is not a program that can be started and left to function; it will rapidly deteriorate without constant monitoring and revitalization.

The major weakness in an itinerant program is the lack of parent-to-parent contact. As noted in the survey of parents of deaf children (Luterman and Kurtzer-White 1998), the biggest felt need of parents, when their child is first diagnosed, is to have contact with other parents. There are elements in the parent-to-parent contact that cannot be duplicated by the professional-parent relationship. Contact with other parents attenuates the loneliness and aloneness that the parents of a newly diagnosed deaf child feels—the emotional support given at home by family and friends is generally directed at trying to make the parents feel better, which only serves to invalidate their feelings and isolate them emotionally. A responsive parent of a deaf child can validate the feelings of a parent whose child has been newly diagnosed with a hearing impairment. An itinerant program cannot stand alone. It must be used in conjunction with intensive short-term programs or center-based ones.

Intense Short-Term Programs

Intensive short-term programs are usually divided into those with strong diagnostic components or those that provide more holistic therapeutic models for the family. Short-term intensive programs serve to complement existing programs, but are not sufficient unto themselves. The Visiting Infant and Parent (V.I.P.) Program at Clarke School is a good example of the short-term intensive program that is basically diagnostic in nature (Gatty 1994) and provides for a comprehensive team evaluation. This particular program is strictly diagnostic with an individual family counseling component as an integral part. Programs such as this can be expanded to include a group experience for parents and children.

The learning vacation experience that was pioneered in Kansas by Miller (1964), and expanded upon at Gallaudet University (Aldridge 1981) is a good example of a comprehensive short-term intensive program that provides both diagnostic and educational components within a recreational setting. I have participated in several "learning vacations" sponsored by schools for the deaf, and have found them to be very valuable. They work especially well with families in rural areas. They allow parents to establish a network, in addition to providing diagnostic teaching for the child. The parent support groups that I facilitated were day-long and very intense as these isolated families suddenly had a forum for expressing long pent-up feelings within an environment of total acceptance. While the parents were in the support group, the children were in diagnostic and recreational activities.

In one program, the learning vacation was a component of the state-wide itinerant program with the parent facilitators also present. They were able to observe the parent group and work within their own support group while the parents were engaged in recreation. Parents, in learning vacation programs, were also provided with information via lectures from staff members.

Center-Based Programs

The most comprehensive programs are usually center based. They frequently provide a team of professionals and can offer an array of services to the family. They usually include audiological testing as well as psychological and educational services. Comprehensive programs will provide nursery and diagnostic teaching for the child to determine the best educational placement, with the parents having a support group experience.

The center-based early intervention programs that I have the most difficulty with are those that are

housed in schools for the deaf. Invariably these programs are methodology driven and are seen as "fun-
nels" into the school. A good early intervention program
needs to be independent of a school and to provide diagnostic teaching for children while empowering parents.
Parents must feel free to go wherever they need to
when their children "graduate" from early intervention.
Administratively, the early intervention component of a
program must not be seen as an extension of a school—
this rarely happens.

One interesting hybrid between the center-based
and the iterant program was the demonstration home
projects that were funded by the Federal Government
in the 1970s. These were home-like structures within
the center—usually a mock living room, kitchen, and
laundry room with cleverly disguised panels that the
instructor could hide behind to instruct the parent. The
teacher and parent would decide beforehand on a
home-based activity such as baking cookies, and the
parent would actually do this while the instructor, from
a hidden vantage point, would coach her on how to use
the activity to provide language stimulation for the
child. These programs had the advantage of providing
center-based activities within a home context and were
almost exclusively parent focused. They seem to have
fallen by the wayside and they should be given another
look because they seem to combine the best features of
the center-based and the itinerant programs.

There are several early intervention programs
that seem able to provide services within the appropriate climate of mutual parent/professional respect: The
D.E.I.P. Program at Boy's Town (Moeller and Condon
1994); the ECHI at the University of Washington
(Thompson 1994); and the Infant Hearing Resource
Program in Portland, Oregon (Rushmer and Schuyler

1994). Unfortunately, many programs begin with a family focus, but, in time, because of inadequate staff training and monitoring, degenerate into a fairly standard, school-driven, methodology-driven model. Moeller and Condon (1994) have commented:

> All too often, programs and professionals have described their approaches to parent/infant intervention as "diagnostic and family centered." Unfortunately, parents involved in early intervention have experienced myriad deficit-focused conversations and endured hundreds of hours of professional modeling. They have often believed their children's progress to be a result of "good schooling," feared that their children's failures were consequences of their own failures and struggled to cope with the unvoiced grief that results from becoming a parent of a child with a disability. . . . Thoughtful, respectful, empowering, productive, family focused early intervention has been the goal of the collaborative problem-solving approach. (p. 168).

It is not enough that programs be in place. It is what transpires within the program that counts. The program that I know best is the one I started over 30 years ago. Here is a description of the program from my chapter in Infants and Toddlers With Hearing Loss (1994), updated and reprinted with permission.

I began working at Emerson College both as an academician teaching undergraduate and graduate courses in audiology and as a clinician in the speech and hearing center associated with the college program. After a few years, I realized that a traditional clinical audiology practice was not for me. In 1965, while casting about for another way to relate to the field, I started—with incredible naivete—a parent-centered nursery program. (I think at times one must leap into the professional void. If one waits to be fully qualified to do something, it is probably too late. A growing professional is always operating on the margins of competency, or incompetency, as the case may be.) It had occurred to me quite early in my professional life that parents of deaf children were not treated well—least of all by me. I knew then that parents needed more help than I could give them in the short-term audiologic counseling sessions I was accustomed to, and also more help than they were able to get from the child-centered programs available to them in the local schools for the deaf. So I conceived a program that was to be a transition for parents as they moved from the diagnosis of their child's hearing loss to entrance into the educational establishment: I wanted to bridge the gap.

Parents of newly diagnosed hearing-impaired children were invited to enroll in the program for an academic year before moving on to a program for the deaf. They were required to come with their child two mornings a week (later increased to three). We insisted that the parents must attend, and that merely "dropping off" the child would not be acceptable. "Parents" were loosely defined to be any primary caregiver. Over the years we have had nannies, grandparents, and aunts bring the child. Occasionally, families have been able to arrange for fathers and mothers to alternate attendance, although most of the time, it has been the mothers who have participated. The nursery room is equipped with a large one-way mirror and observation room. Adjacent to the nursery are several small therapy rooms, also equipped with one-way mirrors and observation rooms. A typical nursery group consists of eight hearing impaired children between the ages of 18 months and 3 years, and one or two normally hearing children—in recent years they have been siblings of the deaf children. There are three components to the program: nursery, individual therapy sessions, and the parent/caregiver support group.

Nursery

One of the many premises upon which the program was founded is that we need to take care of human needs before we can take care of "special" needs. I had met too many "successful" deaf adults who had good oral skills but were unhappy human beings with a limited capacity for joy; I counted them as failures. I did not want to repeat the mistakes of the past, and I wanted to be sure that we treated the children as children first. I hired a nursery teacher who was not a teacher of the deaf. Her task was to keep the staff focused on developmental issues and to remind us that these were children who happened to have a hearing loss. To that end, we also put a hearing child in the nursery (The first one was my third-born child.) The primary reason for doing this was not to provide language stimulation for the deaf children, but to remind all staff and parents what the developmental issues are for a two-year-old. It often seems that there is no creature more deaf on the face of this earth than a two-year old whether he or she has a hearing problem or not. At every age, parents continually confuse developmental issues with deafness issues. In my experience, parents invariably give the child too much credit for being deaf and, therefore, do not discipline the child appropriately. Expectations for the child's behavior are too low, which I think is the biggest obstacle to deaf children realizing their full potential. Low expectations by parents and teachers limit the child severely because people, especially children, have a way of conforming to the expectations of others.

In our program we have never altered the basic notions of keeping the parents as our first responsibility and staying focused on the human needs of parents and children.

Parents are required, in the first few months of the program, to watch the children in the nursery as they interact with our staff and students. The nursery staff is composed of the teacher and several graduate students majoring in speech-language pathology. The staff tries to model effective language intervention strategies within an informal, spontaneous play environment. In the nursery classroom, language is always used in a manner that will give meaning to a child's activities and will fortify the goals of the individual therapy sessions. With an eye toward future years of schooling, some structure is introduced in the form of a daily story hour, snack-time, and activities planned by the students in conjunction with the teacher. A great deal of the learning, however, is accomplished in one-to-one play situations made possible by the number of adults available in the classroom. Our goal is to model for the parents those activities they can engage in at home. One of the rules we have is that no equipment can be purchased for the nursery that is not within monetary budgets of most parents. In the same vein, we do not demonstrate any exotic techniques for parents to use. It is far more useful to show them how an ordinary daily activity, such as having a snack, can become a valuable language learning experience.

After a while (usually six to eight weeks) the parents rotate through the nursery. Because there is a surplus of adults at that point, one student usually observes while the parents work with the remaining nursery staff. We are careful not to let this be seen by the parents as "helping out," but rather as part of their learning experience. There are three routes to learning: you can listen, you can see, or you can do. All three are needed, but the most effective learning is by doing. Keeping parents as passive observers is not enough—they must participate actively in the educational process.

Therapy

Each morning every child receives approximately twenty minutes of individual speech and language intervention. This is a structured, formal session directed to the child's specific language needs. The therapy is provided by second-year graduate students under the supervision of a rehabilitative audiologist. In some years, the supervisor has been a teacher of the deaf. More recently, it has been a rehabilitative audiologist. Here, again, the parents first observe and then gradually take over the session with the interventionist, either in the room or observing through the one-way mirror. We have recently begun to videotape parents conducting "therapy" and have found viewing the tape to be a useful teaching tool. This can only be done after a high level of trust has been established. Toward the end of the academic year, the parents are the primary interventionists. After each session there is a conference to discuss the goals of therapy and what will be happening next. The children are given speech and language tests periodically to determine their progress. Because of the young ages of the children, most testing is done through informal evaluation. Parents periodically fill out a speech-language questionnaire for their child and are encouraged to share the child's home communication attempts with the therapist. In this way, communication goals and the therapy program are determined together by therapists and parents.

Some years we have started parents in therapy by having them teach a child other than their own. Usually the first session with their own child is a disaster; the parent is nervous and wants so badly for the child to perform well that the tension is communicated to the child. Children seldom respond well when we really want them to. In a similar vein, the child has been having so much fun "playing" with the therapist that he or she does not want the parent to intrude. The child often resents the parent's being there and does not mind letting him or her know it.

By having parents start with another child, the initial therapy sessions are often more successful. It also permits them to look more objectively at what that child is doing because they tend to look at their own child with bias. We do not always mix the children and parents in this manner, but we always encourage parents to observe another child in therapy.

During the post therapy conferences, we accent the positive and look at what the parent did well. It is not necessary to tell people what went wrong; they usually know that quite well. We do this in the group session as well, almost never criticizing parents (or students for that matter), but modeling good intervention strategies and supporting the learner at every juncture.

Support Group

One morning a week the parents are required to attend a group session with me as the facilitator. I remember vividly that first session of the first nursery group, and my sitting at the head of the table looking at the anxious, grief-stricken faces of the parents and wondering what in the world I was doing there. I knew I only had a few of the time-worn speeches that had served me well in the short-term contact that typically occurs between audiologists and parents, and I knew they would not serve for the long-term commitment of a support group. An academic year was composed of two fifteen-week semesters, and each group session was ninety minutes in length. I could not fake it for that long, so I had all the parents introduce themselves and tell how they had decided to get involved in the nursery. When everyone had finished, I told them that I didn't know what was supposed to happen in the group, but I hoped that they would be comfortable there. (Actually, I was hoping I would be comfortable there.) A long silence followed as everybody looked around at everybody else. The actual length of silence was probably only thirty seconds, but it felt like hours. Then the parents began to talk to each other; their stories had triggered similar memories in each other. The talk soon became a torrent—I realized, that first day listening to the parents, how lonely they were and that all I needed to do was to bring them together in a safe environment, and they would do all the "work."

In time, I found that the support group became the one place where parents felt they could be understood, where their experiences could be shared. I now know that there is no greater gift that professionals can give to parents than other parents. To do this, professionals must be willing to put aside their set speeches and just listen. Parents will teach you much.

There are certain topics that constantly recur in all groups and, although every group is unique, similar themes run through all of them. At first, parents need to tell their stories. These emerge in the first few sessions. There is usually a great deal of affect in these first few sessions as parents recall the grief and pain of the diagnostic process. One parent's tears usually trigger a like response in other parents. What they are establishing is their credibility. Issues around methodology and hearing aids occupy a considerable amount of time. The dominant emotions in the early stages are fear and grief. Guilt usually emerges somewhat later, as the group develops more trust.

Family issues usually emerge within the first few sessions. Parents invariably are concerned about the effects that deafness has on their marriages, the hearing siblings, and the grandparents. I have found that, after the first few sessions, there are few new topics: the parents merely recycle the ones that emerged early in the life of the group. When a topic re-emerges, parents who were silent the first time contribute, and parents who talked the first time now may add details.

A typical group is composed of the eight parents (usually mothers), two or three graduate students, and, when available, parents of the hearing children. After the first few sessions, I do not allow a new parent into the group. A group rapidly becomes cohesive and develops its own history. When you add a new member, it forces the group to go back to square one. Everyone has to tell his or her story again and trust has to be developed anew. Also, the parents now move fairly quickly past the initial grief reaction, and they resist being taken back by the new parent who is openly grieving, to the uncomfortable place where they had been. They are sympathetic to the pain but unwilling to expose their own pain again. Consequently, the group tends to be static for several sessions until the new member can be assimilated. It is always a setback to have a new member join an ongoing group. Recently, I have modified this "rule" and have been accepting new parents into the group—I am ready to meet the professional challenge posed by trying to integrate a new member into an on-going group—the professional challenge is formidable.

Because our program is based on a two-academic semester model, we refashion the group for the second semester. Parents who applied during the first semester are seen individually and are allowed to enter the group during the second semester. The first-semester college students are replaced by new students. The second semester starts with a reconstituted group that needs to establish its own rules and history.

Parents are not forced to participate in a group. At the outset, it is just assumed that they will. If a parent decides he or she does not want a group experience (most are fearful at first.), he or she can observe child therapy sessions instead.

The group usually becomes the focal point of the program for parents. It is the one place where they can share their feelings and experiences and be understood. The group gives them a feeling of universality. They also get an opportunity within the group to help others, a process that enhances their self-esteem. By using a nondirective strategy (I almost never give them a topic.), I create vacuums that parents must fill. Eventually, they realize that they know more than they thought, and are also more competent than they thought. A group is a powerful vehicle for promoting the growth of parents. I could not conceive of a program without it.

Special Features

Other features of the program also make it valuable to the families we serve. Some of these features we started at the beginning, whereas others have been added over the years.

Deafness is very much a family affair, and programs have to afford options for the whole family's participation. We have evolved several.

Saturday Nursery Once each semester we hold nursery on a Saturday to allow participation of family members who might otherwise not be able to attend. Usually, the fathers attend, but the extended families of aunts, uncles, and grandparents are also included. This gives them all a chance to see the child in the nursery and in individual sessions, and a chance to talk with the staff. While the staff invariably grumbles about giving up a Saturday, it is generally acknowledged afterward that these sessions are very worthwhile.

Grandparents' Day   One of the Saturdays, usually in the spring, we designate as Grandparents' Day. We ask the parents to make a special effort to get the grandparents to attend because, in addition to observing the group and individual sessions, we try to form a Grandparent Group. The grandparents have a unique perspective on the child's deafness and its effects on the family—it is double hit for them—they are grieving for their grandchild as well as for their own child's pain. Grandparents usually get locked into denial and often resent receiving information secondhand from their adult children. Frequently, there is a lot of tension within the family created by the grandparents' denial and the lack of communication between parent and grandparent.

Grandparents are frequently seen as a burden rather than an asset. They are also incredibly lonely, rarely having opportunities to talk to other grandparents of deaf youngsters. It is hard to assemble a grandparent group. They usually live away from their children or spend several months of the year in warmer climates. Many are too infirm to travel to our center.

Whenever we have a large number of grandparents living in the vicinity of the nursery, we hold a parent/grandparent evening meeting. At these times, I have used a fish bowl design very effectively. In this design, the grandparents are in the center of the circle while the parents are on the outside. (Only people on the inside can talk.) I start the session with a question such as "What is it like to be the grandparent of a deaf child?" After 45 minutes of discussion, the groups reverse with grandparents on the outside and the parents on the inside. I start the parents' discussion with a parallel question of "What is it like to be the parent of a deaf child?" Afterward, we form a large circle and everyone discusses the experience. This design mandates listening; it is sometimes much easier to hear someone other than your own child or your parent. I have also found this design useful in groups consisting of husband/wife or parent/professional dyads.

Sibling Day   All siblings are affected by the presence of a deaf child in the family, and they, too, need professional attention. We always allow siblings to come to the nursery with their parent; if the parent is willing to supervise the child, sibling attendance is encouraged. We no longer set aside a designated day for brothers and sisters (as we did in the past), rather our sibling education is ongoing.

Because the deaf children in our program are so young (birth to three years), the siblings are usually also quite young. Rarely do we find a family with hearing adolescents. Because of this, we have not had a sibling group session, although we would certainly be open to one. Siblings need a chance to talk with other siblings, in much the same way as the adults need each other.

Evening Meetings   Evening meetings are held for spouses who cannot attend during the day. This is usually the father, but occasionally the group includes a mother or two. These groups meet infrequently and seldom develop the cohesiveness we find in the weekly support group. We usually hold only one or two evening meetings a semester. A fathers-only group is rarely emotional in the overt way that a mothers' group is. The men usually prefer to stick with the nuts and bolts of deafness, although some groups are surprisingly open and forthcoming. There is a subtle chemistry of groups that the leader has no control over—groups must be taken as they come.

We always give parents their choice of format and frequency of evening meetings. They can be fathers-only groups or husband/wife groups. In husband/wife groups there is usually more restraint because neither spouse wants to pay a heavy price for what is said in public. For a few heady years, we were flush with money and were able to take parents away for a weekend without children. Within the confines of limited time and space, the groups developed a great deal of intimacy. The fish bowl design was very powerful. Those husband/wife groups became the most powerful groups we have had. (During the past several years, I have been facilitating parent learning vacations for other programs. I also find them to be the most powerful group sessions I do. When people are out of their traditional environments and roles, with a severe time limitation, they are apt to risk more.)

Day Off Several times each semester, we give the parents a day off. We tell them to leave the child and to do something for themselves. This sends an important message to the parents that they need to take time for themselves. One of our themes is that happy parents produce happy kids. Taking time for themselves periodically enables them to be able to give quality time to their children. I often tell parents that when I travel by air, the stewardess reminds me that if I am accompanied by a child and the oxygen mask should fall down, I should put the mask on my face first, then the child's. As nurturers/providers, we need to take care of ourselves first in order to be able to take care of our children. The periodic day-off conveys to the parents our programmatic support for that notion.

Infant Program   During the first decade or two of the program, we rarely saw a child under 18 months of age. We are now getting referrals for many children under one year of age. I think there is an increased awareness of deafness as a diagnostic possibility on the part of the medical profession, which has occurred as angry parents have gone back to pediatricians and apprised them of their errors. There is also an increased use of auditory brainstem testing in our geographic area, and deaf children are often identified sooner. In addition it is now mandatory in our state for hearing testing to be provided for all newborns in intensive care units as part of the high-risk register, and the screening of newborns has begun in several hospitals.

On the day that the support group meets, the parents of newly identified infants come as well. We provide baby sitting for the children while their parents participate in the support group. The infants and their parents are seen once a week for individual sessions with a rehabilitative audiologist and a graduate student. As the infants mature and are able to participate in the nursery, the parents enter the regular program.

Content Acquisition   On the days when parents observe in the nursery, we also offer miniseminars. During the past few years, we have offered a signing class for those parents who wish to attend. Occasionally, the audiologist will meet with parents to discuss testing procedures or hearing aids. The nursery school teacher may also meet with parents to discuss topics such as discipline or toilet training. All topics emerge from parent interest—we rarely impose a topic, but ask the parents what interests them.

Occasionally, I do lecture on specific topics in the parent support groups, but that invariably arises spontaneously from parental concern. Moreover, I have a book collection that I circulate among the parents, because I prefer that they work a bit for the information that they need. The groups themselves become highly informative as parents share with one another information they have acquired. The information is much more valuable to parents when they have learned it for themselves. It also boosts their self-esteem enormously when they are able to supply information to others.

Admission Procedures   From the outset, we have been interested in seeing only those families who choose us. Choice, when made freely, always involves a greater commitment. To that end, we developed a passive admissions procedure. We do not accept a third-party referral; parents must call us. I encourage them to come and see the program in action. Then I explain that it is a parent-centered program and the emphasis is on them (they usually don't hear this.) I give them an application form and the name and telephone numbers of parents who are either currently enrolled in the program or are "graduates." I also give them a directory of other programs in the area and urge them to consider other options. I never follow up on the initial visit. If the parents do not send in the application, I assume that they have found another one more suitable. We have never denied admission to any parent who wished to attend our program.

As a consequence of our admission policy, we have tended to deal with middle-class or upwardly mobile parents who are already actively involved in their child's education. It is a self-selecting group. Over the years, we have had a low drop-out rate. Most families complete the program and many are reluctant to leave. We also recognize that a family-centered program is not for everyone—communities and facilities must offer a variety of program options without valuing any one program more than others. Parents will select what is best for them, if we allow them to make choices. It is my firm belief that if a program tries to do everything for everybody, it will either fail or doom itself to mediocrity.

Special Issues

Early intervention programs must address the following issues.

Methodology

In our program, parents are given a choice of methods. We believe that no method will be effective unless the parents themselves choose it. The only way this will happen is if they make the choice and commit themselves to it. In the very early stages, parents often will not have a clear idea of what methods they prefer. If an infant has a profound loss and the parents cannot decide, we will suggest an auditory/oral approach with supplementary use of signs. For children with significant residual hearing, we will always start a child using an auditory/oral approach.

The methodology issue is discussed at length in the support group. The program affords parents ample opportunity to look at their child objectively (or as objectively as any parent can) in the observation room while our staff interacts with him or her. They also have a chance to compare their child's progress with others. They can request a change of method at any point.

Our philosophy of methodology is that if a particular approach works well for one child and family, it is good for them but not necessarily appropriate for others. At all times, we try to fit the method to the child, rather than the child to the method. We often tell parents that the child will "tell" us how he or she wants to learn because some children are more verbal and others more gestural by nature. We offer the parents the option of auditory/oral, cued speech, and total communication. To date, we have had no parents request that we use American Sign Language exclusively, without emphasizing hearing aids and speech. If a family should express a desire to use ASL exclusively, we would refer them to another program. Although ASL deserves recognition as an appropriate language for deaf adults, I cannot, in good conscience, offer ASL as an option for very young deaf children. Try as I might, I still see deafness as a disability that can be minimized by the appropriate use of technology, consistent methodology, and good parent education. I do not see ASL as a feasible option for most hearing parents primarily because they do not become so competent in ASL that it becomes the "mother tongue." I also feel strongly that the goal of early intervention should be to give the child as many choices as possible, and then to respect the choices eventually made. ASL, by limiting the use of hearing aids and oral communication, is, in my view, a very restrictive option. As professionals, we need to have clear limits on what we will do, and although I have broad areas of accommodation, there are times I refuse to accommodate, because to do so would compromise my own core values.

We hold an evening meeting in the spring semester in which parents get a chance to meet deaf adults. In the early years of the program, the deaf panel was selected almost randomly. Unfortunately, we usually had at least one angry deaf adult who would lecture the parents on the virtues of ASL and signing. He or she would invariably upset the parents who had opted for an auditory/oral route and cause unnecessary guilt in all the parents. During the last several years, we have had panels consisting of graduates from our program accompanied by their parents. I select the panel carefully so that there are children who have elected an oral route and others who have opted to sign. I also try to pick mainstreamed children as well as children who have been educated in schools for the deaf. The parents of the children are there to add a much needed parental perspective. This meeting is always well attended and is very successful in promoting a thoughtful consideration of the methodology issues.

Deaf Parents

On rare occasions we have had deaf parents of deaf children attend the nursery. Generally, this has not been successful. Deaf parents respond very differently to having a deaf child than do hearing parents (Halpern 1989). They rarely have a grief reaction. One father said to me, "I'm glad my child is deaf. I wouldn't know how to raise a hearing child."

The major difficulty I encountered with deaf parents was in the support group. The presence of a deaf mother restricted the hearing mothers, making it difficult for them to voice their dismay at their child's deafness. Every time they did, the deaf mother would say, in effect, "Deafness isn't so bad, look at me." The parents would look at her and what they saw was an adult with barely intelligible speech who had to rely on an interpreter. But they could not express their pain openly—it would not be considered "polite"—and, at that time, I lacked the skills needed to elicit their feelings.

I know now that if we have a deaf parent in a group with hearing parents, I will have to confront the whole group on how they are feeling about the deaf parent. This would be uncomfortable for everyone, but it would be necessary in order to encourage the kind of openness a group needs to function properly.

In the early stages of coping, parents move from denial to resistance. In resistance, they bolster themselves with the belief that their child will be a special case—a super-oral adult who can pass for hearing. In this early stage, most parents are not ready to meet a non-oral deaf adult. Programs have to be sensitive to this; it is very difficult to work with a mixed group of parents. This also means one should not rush to have parents of newly diagnosed deaf children meet deaf adults; later, they will be better prepared to meet them as they should.

I have worked with a group of deaf parents of deaf children; however, this group had very little emotion and it remained problem focused. Its members wanted specific information on child rearing and availability of assistance. Because they had already come to terms with their own deafness, they felt no need to discuss methodology or feelings. I do not sign and all communication was conducted through an interpreter. I was very uncomfortable using an interpreter, as I was missing the nuances of communication so necessary to facilitate growth and learning. Perhaps a facilitator who was a fluent signer could have done more.

Funding

Funding is a chronic problem. The first several years of the nursery were fully supported by a United States Office of Education Demonstration Grant. There were no fees for the parents. In subsequent years, the program was fully supported by the college for training purposes and as a community outreach facility. (It was good public relations.) When the college could no longer support the program entirely, we instituted a fee scaled to ability to pay, but no one was ever denied service for financial reasons. The fee, if paid in full, would still not cover the full cost of the program and, while we are still subsidized in part by the college, a sizable funding gap must be filled each year. This gap is filled by philanthropy; both private and corporate alumni and friends of the college have been donors. Recently, early intervention programs have contracted with us for our services which has provided us with a steady stream of income. There have been years when I was sure we would not be able to continue, and then an angel appeared. Somehow, we have survived from one year to the next. If a program fills a need, then clients and donors always find their way to its door.

Keeping Focused

The hardest thing to do in the program is to keep the focus on parents. It is easy to get seduced by the children. They are so appealing that professionals often tend to put children as the center of their attention. In order for a family-focused program to work, professional attention must be on parents, not easy to do when the children are so "seductive".

We encourage focus on parents by asking our staff to write "lesson plans" for the parents rather than for the children. Everyone must see children as the raw material from which parents can learn. It is difficult for a staff member to sit in the observation room and watch a mother fumble through a communication interaction with "her child." Professionals must lose their fear of parents (students are always much more fearful of parent evaluations than they are of their supervisors.) It is hard to encourage students to talk with parents after nursery sessions; it usually takes an entire semester for them to become relaxed around parents.

Parents, themselves, do not always appreciate the parent-centered program, preferring to keep the child in the forefront.There is a strong tendency on the part of parents to "let the professionals do it." It is so much easier to sit back and watch rather than actually do, a tendency born out of parental insecurities. Our aim is to empower parents and thus build their self-esteem. They often prefer not to participate at this level. We are flexible and loving, but firm in our insistence that all parents participate directly in the early intervention process.

Program Coordination

In order to be successful, it is absolutely essential that all the program elements be coordinated. For example, we coordinate individual sessions and the nursery by having a "goal box." Graduate student clinicians write out their goals for the children and leave them in the box in the nursery. The nursery staff reviews these objectives weekly, and each member works on each child's goals during the spontaneous play that the nursery provides. These goals are developed in conjunction with the parents, also.

The entire staff meets weekly, usually after a parent support group meeting, to discuss each family. Graduate students participate in the support group and report on what happened that day so that everyone knows what is occurring at the parent level. The children are also reviewed by nursery staff and therapists.

Staff

The staff is the most critical aspect of the program. A program such as ours cannot succeed unless all staff members share the basic family-centered philosophy of the program. This is not to say that there are never disagreements, but the core philosophy must be in harmony. Each program has its own "culture" and everyone must agree with it in order for there to be consistency within the program.

In selecting staff, I am not impressed by titles or curriculum vitae. I want people who are vital and interested in others but willing to take risks and who care deeply about what they are doing. Over the years, I have hired speech-language pathologists, audiologists, nursery school teachers, parents, and an assortment of people with unusual backgrounds. Some have not worked out well and have left quickly. For our type of program, the key to staff selections is to identify people who are nurturing, but not smothering. In effect, what happens within the program is that the staff becomes parents to the parents; we try to model effective intervention strategies by how we interact with family members. Therefore, it is essential for us to select only staff members capable of being nurturing human beings.

Staff and program culture are much more important than facilities. Our nursery was in a remodeled garage that was built before insulation was considered important. Consequently, we all froze during the winter and sweltered during the summers, yet we consistently turned out successful groups of parents and children. Recently, we moved to luxurious quarters that include air conditioning and heat. I am not sure our "product" is any better, although we are more comfortable.

We have made several attempts to try to evaluate the results of the program. One cannot design a rigorous scientific study to compare graduates of this program with graduates of child-centered programs in the area because the families are so different. I do know from a recent survey we did to commemorate the 25th anniversary of the program that there are many parents who are very grateful for having had a chance to participate in the program. Over the years, I have learned the following:

If you take good care of the parents, the children turn out fine.

You cannot go any faster than the parent is ready to go, and you can't save children from their parents.

Parents are smart and will choose well for themselves if given the chance. They are the only ones with the full picture.

There are no intervention techniques more powerful than those that serve to build parental self-esteem.

If you treat everyone in the program with loving respect, they will grow.

Never pity the parents; empathize with their pain and arm yourself with the knowledge that if you allow them to struggle, they will emerge with increased strength. Deafness is a powerful teacher for everyone.

CHAPTER 4

Early Intervention: Revisiting Therapy

Ellen Kurtzer-White

In the 1970s, I packed a typewriter and other essentials for graduate school into a rusting yellow Fiat and headed south toward Tennessee. There were federal dollars sufficient for my training at a prestigious institution with a demonstration teaching home for children with communication disorders near the university's hearing and speech center. With a curriculum that offered a "focus in early intervention," the program was the first step on my way to a career of working with hearing impaired children—once I had the requisite coursework, clinical experiences, and credentials. I graduated secure in my beliefs that children were the focus of intervention, and that profoundly deaf preschoolers could (should) develop oral language (after all, I had heard deaf children speak with southern accents) if only their parents would keep their hearing aids on and comply with professional recommendations.

One of my first positions was at a private school for the deaf that provided a total communication environment in which the staff simultaneously spoke and used a form of signed English, and children wore amplification devices. This first exposure to manual English systems, along with issues of clear and consistent "access to language," was a catalyst for a personal change of mind. Working daily with preschoolers who had developed language and communication skills through signing was sufficient evidence for me to revise my opinion of what was best for deaf children, if only their parents would learn sign language at a pace two steps ahead of their child and remember that amplification still was important.

Committed to the importance of signing in the acquisition of English, I became the school audiologist at another, larger state school for the deaf. I believed that signing did not preclude the development of oral language skills, but facilitated and enhanced it— that deaf children needed consistent use of functioning and appropriate amplification, speech therapy, and consistent access to language through sign. Yet the issue of parent compliance remained, despite families' sincere desires to fully communicate with their children and ultimately to have them speak.

With hindsight, I now see that although I have always intended to be a sensitive, empathic professional, my posture along the way has been at times presumptuous and patronizing. Certain instances come quickly to mind. There was a family who had driven hours from Kentucky to Nashville with their beautiful deaf school-aged daughter. I spent hours teaching her mother how to speak to her child, how to point out sounds in the environment, how to elicit speech sounds, and how to change the batteries in the hearing aids. I did not know until much later that the sole income producer in the family, the child's father, was a coal miner on strike. All the activities and techniques I had demonstrated were irrelevant to the daily crises this family faced, even though they were consistent with my professional role and the needs of the child as defined in a child-centered model. I never raised the question of what the family truly needed from me. The assumption was that they had come to me for answers and I knew exactly what they should be doing at home.

There was a well-educated, articulate couple whose eighteen-month-old daughter became profoundly deaf as a result of meningitis. They were devastated to think of their daughter as being unable to talk. After hours of home visits and discussions about the impact such profound hearing loss would have on spoken language, social, and cognitive development, these parents continued to be "resistant" to accepting our opinion that an oral approach would be extraordinarily difficult, if not impossible, for their child. At a time when cochlear implants were in their infancy technologically, the family pursued this option for their daughter despite our skepticism. The child underwent the surgery and the family moved away to enroll her in an oral school. Many years later, I heard this girl's incredibly intelligible, fluent speech and was grateful that her parents had not listened to my "expert opinion."

These families were important teachers for me. They helped me redefine my role as a professional and as an interventionist. I have learned that although I have expertise and information, I cannot assume the role of decision maker, of telling parents what they ultimately should do. Each family has its unique set of values, needs, and priorities that must be acknowledged and respected. Had I established an intervention plan with the family at the center rather than myself as the professional who knew best; had I asked the right questions, listened to, and valued the responses, the families and children could have benefited more from our time together.

The clinical landscape has changed dramatically in the twenty years since my graduate-school days, and so has the way I work with families whose babies are deaf. The child-centered intervention approach of the 1970s has been replaced by family-centered programming, with the realization that deafness has an impact not only on the child, but on the entire family (Luterman 1987). The child is viewed as part of a system of parents, siblings, and grandparents who live within an even larger system of social networks and community. Family-focused programming views parents as competent, responsible decision makers who, with support and information from unbiased, non-judgmental professionals, will make their own best choices. A healthy, more productive relationship between family and professional emerges when a professional truly listens and plans according to family priorities. Ultimately, children benefit from good relationships between clinicians and parents.

Research and technology have brought the goals of early identification and intervention closer to reality, with the ultimate benchmark of reducing, if not preventing, the language and communication delays associated with childhood deafness (Yoshinaga-Itano et al. 1996). More families with very young babies are entering early intervention systems. Early no longer means toddlers, it means infants. Traditional services that may have met the needs of families in the past need to be carefully reassessed. What may have worked for older babies may not work for infants and their families. In fact, there is little scientific data or research to guide us in working with this newly created clinical population.

Careful research in speech perception, speech production, and language development of infants with significant hearing loss, along with the psychological/emotional impact of early diagnosis on parents and family, is needed. Until results are available, we must draw upon the established developmental sequences in the early communication of children with normal hearing and the known characteristics of hearing families with young deaf children.

This chapter discusses three critical components in the system of normal communication development: 1) caregiver influences, 2) infant capacities and development, and 3) the social interactive context in which early communication occurs. The impact deafness has on those components is reviewed, and traditional models of intervention and their inherent limitations are analyzed. A new model of intervention that integrates the three components of early communication is proposed.

Early Communication Development

Hearing children are born into an environment that is an exquisite system of dynamic, interdependent, and interactive processes that occur within the child and also between the child and important people and events in the child's environment. These processes allow language acquisition to take place in an almost unconscious, intuitive, and automatic way. Children come "equipped" with perceptual, motor, cognitive, linguistic, and social-emotional capabilities that develop in predictable sequences over time, as well as an intrinsic motivation to communicate and to become competent language users. Parents and caregivers communicate with babies in highly specialized ways, with strong beliefs that babies are capable of communicating. This belief and adult responsiveness to the child's developing communicative behaviors are essential to the development of successful, spoken communication. This system of communication development is far greater than the sum of all its parts. Consequently, a breakdown in any one of the components results in a breakdown of the whole system. To understand early communication, then, requires an understanding of the contributing constituents of the system as well as their interactions and connections: caregiver influences such as adult sensitivity, responsivity, and contingency; infant communicative capacities and stages of development; and the social context of the interaction.

Caregiver Influences

Adults who care for babies are usually competent language users and motivated play and conversational partners. The language they use, how and when they communicate, and the social framework within which communication occurs affects the child's language development. Adults' interpretation and response to infant behaviors "allows babies a way into the language system, helping them to learn to express real intentions." (Stark 1991).

Sensitivity, Responsivity, and Contingency   Caregivers and babies interact and communicate in a transactional way, each influencing the other's communicative behavior and response (McLean 1990; Prizant and Wetherby 1993; Sacks 1989). Before an infant intends to or is able to truly communicate, caregivers respond to the child's most primitive, reflexive vocalizations as if they were in fact intentional (Dunst, Lowe, and Bartholomew 1990; Mc Lean 1990; Snow 1976, 1982). Simply put, adults act as if the child meant to say something long before he or she does. For example, parents interpret an infant's cry of distress as, "Oh, you want your bottle." The adult belief that babies can and do communicate meaningfully is critical for communicative development throughout the language-learning years (McLean 1990).

Caregiver contingent responsiveness also influences language development (Dunst, Lowe, and Bartholomew 1990). An adult response is considered contingent when it is directly linked to a baby's signals and the context of the interaction, whether the response is to certain sounds, gestures, facial expressions, or to later development of words and language. When an adult offers a predictable and relevant response, a baby's communicative behavior is reinforced. A baby learns to signal in a consistent way that is clearly readable to an adult, and an adult's predictable response becomes readable to the child. Contingency also requires the adult to be sensitive to the child's focus of attention and to respond accordingly.

When caregivers respond to a child's behavior, they provide linguistic mapping (Warren and Yoder 1998), an appropriate language model relevant to whatever seems to be holding the baby's attention. A baby gazes at the mobile above the crib and the parent provides the relevant words. "There's the bunny. It goes round and round. Here comes the duck," and so on. The baby reaches for a toy, and again the adult provides the relevant text. In this way, following a child's lead and sharing the attentional focus positively influences language acquisition (Wilcox and Shannon 1998). Following a child's lead also facilitates language development because a child's involvement in the activity or social interaction tends to be longer and the quality of a child's attention greater when adults respond sensitively (Warren and Yoder 1998).

In summary, adults help to ensure successful communication when they follow a child's attentional lead, are responsive to a baby's communicative behaviors, offer contingent responses, and rephrase or model language appropriate to the context. They help a child to be an active participant in communication and reinforce the child's motivation to gain information about language and to become identified with it.

Child-Directed Speech   The special type of speech used when interacting with a young child is critical. Initially labeled motherese, this highly stylized communication is now referred to as child-directed speech and has several characteristics that describe it (Snow 1976; Menyuk, Liebergott and Schultz 1995). Adults are neither conscious of nor do they plan the ways they modify their communication to young children (Menyuk, Lie bergott, and Schultz 1995). Child-directed speech is clearer, slower, more fluent, and has more pauses than adult-directed speech. Facial expression and prosody are exaggerated. The speech is phonologically simple and higher in pitch with a broader, richer intonation. Important words in the sentence are stressed, making vowels longer and louder. Ends of sentences are marked by rising intonations, and pauses mark the boundaries between phrases or clauses (Menyuk, Liebergott, and Schultz 1995). Salient acoustic cues in child-directed speech may help make it easier for infants to acquire phonology (sound system), lexicon (words), and syntax (the rules for putting words together for different meanings) (Menyuk, Liebergott, and Schultz 1995).

Child-directed speech also provides important linguistic information. Caregivers systematically fine-tune their speech and language to match the child's level (McLean 1990; Snow 1976). For example, adults tend to speak to infants in shorter, simpler sentences and provide a solid scaffold that supports the infant as he/she tries to take a turn. Adults use simple language, in terms of meaning and grammar (Snow 1976; Schirmer 1994), as well as a significant number of questions and repetitions. The topic is rooted in the "here and now," that is, related to the current interaction. As a baby develops words and language, an adult will systematically "up the linguistic ante" in response to the child, showing the way to the next language stage. Parents help young children learn language structures, not only by modeling, but by rephrasing and expanding upon the child's utterances. For example, in one context, an adult's response to a child's "doggie" may be "Yes, that's a big doggie. The doggie is happy. He's wagging his tail. Pat the doggie."

Infant Communicative Capacities

Speech Perception

Exactly how babies acquire language through what they hear is not yet fully understood. What is known is that at birth, babies have fully developed cochleae and a neural network capable of transmitting acoustic signals to specific areas of the brain. Infants are "wired for sound," particularly for the sounds of their mothers' voices. Within weeks after birth, infants demonstrate a preference for their mother's voice over other female speakers (DeCasper and Fifer 1980) as well as for infant directed speech (Cooper and Aslin 1994). They perceive incredibly minute acoustic changes in speech, such as, differences of milliseconds (e.g., voice onset time) that can change the meanings of words (Eimas 1974). Infants can discriminate supraseg-mental aspects (the "melody" of speech, such as the rising intonation of a question or the falling intonation of a phrase or sentence), as well as the rhythmic or melodic patterns of speech that distinguish speakers and languages (Jusczyk 1995). Infants are initially able to discriminate speech sounds within their native language as well as in non-native languages (Jusczyk 1995). By the second half of their first year, babies' discrimination of foreign speech contrasts diminishes as they become more attuned to the sounds and sequences of sounds that occur in their native language (Kuhl et al. 1992; Morgan and Saffran 1995).

The salient acoustic cues in speech may help babies learn to segment the blur of running speech into meaningful pieces. In order to make sense of, and ultimately acquire oral language, babies must discover the rules for how meaningful components are put together: which sounds can go together, which rhythmic patterns make words, and how words go together to form phrases and sentences (Morgan 1996). They need to recognize and locate words in fluent speech in order to understand the meanings within an utterance. This is an amazing and complex task, since the shapes of sounds and words can change when they come in contact with each other (Morgan 1996). That is, the acoustics of a speech sound produced in isolation may change when that sound is put into a syllable. The acoustics of a syllable may change when it is put into a word, and the acoustics of a word can change when it is put into a phrase or sentence.

Babies first perceive the whole of what is said and move through developmental sequences within their abilities to segment. They are sensitive to acoustic cues for clauses at 4 to 6 months, phrases at about 9 months, and word units at about 11 months (Menyuk, Liebergott, and Schultz 1995). With experience, they also perceive the distribution of sounds (i.e., how often certain aspects of speech occur) which may help them to figure out word boundaries (Morgan and Saffran 1995). Babies' discrimination abilities for segments and suprasegments develop from the general to the specific (Menyuk, Liebergott, and Schultz 1995). In learning oral language, babies do not add up discrete phonemes to make words, such as d+o+g = dog. In addition, they are not passive recipients of adult input nor do they merely imitate. Babies actively listen and strategize to "crack the code." They find patterns and test out hypotheses to figure out the system.

Stages in Infant Communicative Development

Infant communicative development is a system unto itself. Table I was compiled from numerous models and research results (Dunst, Wortman, and Bartholomew 1990; McLean 1990; Morgan 1996; Oller 1980, 1994; Stark 1991; Stark, Bernstein, and Demorest 1993) to provide a broader perspective and systems view. Rather than focusing exclusively on one aspect, such as production or perception as a linear process, several processes that co-occur at certain points in a young child's life are presented. The table is a guide for the stages and developmental sequences across many domains: infant vocal development; the functions of vocal behavior; the development of auditory perception; and the communicative significance of each stage.

The reader is reminded of several important points about the information presented in the table.

Table I Developmental sequences of co-occurring processes in early communication: vocal production and function, speech perception, and early communicative/linguistic significance.

Vocal Development[1]	Vocal Behavior/Function[2]	Auditory Perception[3]	Communicative Significance[4]
Stage I (0–2 months) Phonation • nonspeech-like; • burps, sneezes, etc.	Stage I (0–2 months) Reflexive Sound Making	• perceives all speech sounds • prefers mother's voice	Infant: • develops consistent signals • responds to prosody Adult: • interprets signals as meaningful • provides prosodic input
Stage 2 (1–4 months) Primitive Articulation (Cooing/gooing) • series of prolonged phonation • back vowels and consonants /ku/, /gu/ • nasals • primitive /k/, /g/ • mostly vowels	Stage 2 (2–5 months) Reactive Sound Making occurs until 10 months	• begins to discriminate and recognize emotional intent based on prosodic features	Infant: • engages in early social interaction • vocalizes to adults, objects • produces more syllables if turn-taking with adult • is not intentional, but communicates more purposefully Adult: • interprets signals as intents • maps language
Stage 3 (4–6 months) Expansion • raspberries, yells • vowel-like sounds	Stage 3 (3–5 months) Activity Sound Making	• prefers infant-directed language (4–5 months) • is sensitive to clause boundaries (4–6 months)	Infant: • produces sounds with sensorimotor activity • is not intentional

Table I *continued*

Vocal Development[1]	Vocal Behavior/Function[2]	Auditory Perception[3]	Communicative Significance[4]
• vocal play			Adult: • interprets baby's vocalizations and signals as intents
Stage 4 (5–10 months) Canonical Syllable • limited speech sounds • strings of CV syllables • reduplicated /mamama/ • variegated /dadi/ • mid-front lax vowels • /m, b, d/	Stage 4 (6–9 months) Activity Sound Making	• prefers appropriately segmented, infant directed native speech/language (5–9 months) • observes differences between rising/falling intonation • responds differentially to speech vs nonspeech stimuli (6 months) • uses auditory feedback • relates sound stimulus to sound making object (8–10 months)	Infant: • produces sounds with sensorimotor activity • produces rhythmic, repetitive sounds • is not intentional Adult: • interprets baby's vocalizations and signals as intents
Stage 5 (9–18 months) Integrative • vowels /i/ /u/ • vowels and dipthongs • stops, glides • CV syllables	Stage 5 (9–18 months) Communicative Sound Making • Regulatory • Personal • Interactional	9 months: • segments words • discriminates speech contrasts • discriminates prosodic contrasts	9–12 months: Infant: communicates intentionally for a range of functions: -request -showing -protest

Table I *continued*

Vocal Development[1]	Vocal Behavior/Function[2]	Auditory Perception[3]	Communicative Significance[4]
• variegated babbling • new intonation contours • first words • babbling + words • first words • babbling + words	• Heuristic/Imaginative (Halliday)	• prefers sound sequences, words and rhythm patterns of native language • comprehends limited words and phases within context • is sensitive to word boundaries (11 months) • has receptive vocabulary of about 50 words (12 months)	–comment • moves from gesture and sounds to words and symbolic language Adult: • fine tunes input; increases length and complexity • models and expands language • provides semantic contingencies

The reader is reminded that the ages of the sequences are highly variable, however, the sequences of development are not.

[1]Oller 1994; Stoel-Gammon 1998

[2]Stark 1991; Stark, Bernstein, and Demorest 1993

[3]Eimas, 1974; Jusczyk 1995; Jusczyk, Cutler, and Rednaz 1993; Jusczyk, Luce, and Charles-Luce 1994; Morgan 1996; Morgan and Saffram 1995; Menyuk, Leibergot, and Schultz 1995

[4]Dunst, Worman Lowe, and Bartholomew 1990; McLean 1990; Menyuk 1974; Menyuk, Liebergot, and Schultz 1995; Schirmer 1994

The ages at which babies move through developmental sequences is highly variable; however, the order of the sequences is not. The emphasis is on the predictable milestones of development, not the specific age of acquisition of particular stages. The stages are fluid: the child does not simply cross the border from one to the next. Development is a process that sometimes includes both forward and backward movement. A baby who appears to have moved into a new stage may still hold on to behaviors that are more consistent with an earlier one.

In the beginning: Stage I (0 to about 2 months)   Oller (1980, 1994) describes the first stage of vocal development as "phonation." A baby begins to produce sounds at birth: cries, burps, and other reflexive noises, as well as vowel-like sounds. Baby noises in this reflexive sound-making stage do not seem like speech, nor are they communicative or intentional (Stark, Bernstein, and Demorest 1993). Caregivers, however, interpret these sounds as meaningful. An adult hearing an infant wail is likely to think the baby is crying for a bottle or a clean diaper, when, in fact, the child may be crying from distress. Sounds made when an infant is visually stimulated by a patterned mobile may be interpreted as, "You like that. So pretty." The adult responds and offers simple yet prosodically salient language appropriate to the situation and contingent upon the baby's behavior. The baby perceives the prosody. The adult's contingent and repeated responses reinforce and help the baby learn to make consistent and clear signals. In this example, the baby learns that when he or she cries, an adult with a soothing voice will come and offer food or comfort. The baby becomes readable to the caregiver and the caregiver readable to the infant.

Several important contributing factors to successful communication development are already being established in this newborn period: (1) Adults believe the baby is capable of communicating and interpret the baby's behaviors as if they were meaningful; (2) Adults offer contingent responses; (3) Baby and adults are mutually affecting each other's behavior and their signals are becoming more readable for each other; (4) Parents intuitively modify their communication with the baby; (5) Baby is predisposed to listen to the adult speech directed toward infants; and (6) Acoustic cues are meaningful to the infant. The continuation and evolution of these processes throughout subsequent stages of communication are essential to development.

Stage 2 The earliest major landmark in vocal development is cooing (Stark 1991). At about 7 to 8 weeks, infants begin to produce a series of prolonged, more speechlike sounds: back vowels, nasals, and the primitive consonants /k/ and /g/. During this stage of reactive sound making (Stark, Bernstein, and Demorest 1993), babies are particularly vocal when gazing at an object (e.g., a mobile) for a long time or in face-to-face interaction with a smiling adult. Vocal behaviors are paired with interactive behaviors of mutual gaze. This early form of social interaction is a basis for turn taking in language. The pleasant back and forth exchanges of cooing between baby and adult is an early form of conversation. Each partner has a chance to "speak" and to wait his or her turn.

Caregiver response helps shape the baby's production. Three-month-old infants were found to be more vocal and to produce a greater percentage of syllables when adults waited for their turn to respond, and when they provided the baby with a verbal response (Stoel-Gammon 1998).

Stage 3 Babies move into an expansion stage of vocal development at about 3 to 8 months (Oller 1994). This is a time of vocal play when infants experiment with the kinds of sounds they can make, such as squeals, yells, and raspberries. Long series of vowel-like and consonant-like sounds emerge (Stark 1991) and some syllable sounds are produced. These vocalizations occur almost entirely when babies are engaged in sensori-motor activity (e.g., mouthing, crawling, cruising, exploring, and manipulating objects) and rarely result from adult interaction (Stark 1991). Activity sound making continues until about age 9 months.

At around 3 months, babies are able to discriminate sequences that convey different intents (Menyuk, Liebergott, and Schultz 1995). At about 4 to 6 months, babies become sensitive to acoustic cues that mark clauses (Menyuk, Liebergott, and Schultz 1995). In other words, they begin to recognize when sentences begin and end, as well as the emotional intent of the utterance.

Stage 4 The production of true syllables (i.e., having the same timing characteristics as adult syllables) that are consonant-vowel or vowel-consonant units, referred to as canonical (Oller 1980), emerges at around 6 months and continues until about 12 months. Canonical babbling occurs when babies produce strings of syllables, such as /mamama/, and, later, variegated syllables such as /ba da/ (Stark, Bernstein, and Demorest 1993). Speech sounds at this time typically include stops, nasals, glides, and lax vowels.

At this stage, babies' physical movements are rhythmical and repetitive; so are the vocal sounds. Rhythm also plays a part in a baby's speech perception. At 6 months, infants appear biased toward attending to rhythmic properties of speech rather than segmental ones (Morgan 1996). They are listening to the rhythms of sound patterns in the adult speech directed to them—phrases and words—not individual sounds. Babies may also be listening to themselves, since auditory feedback is considered necessary for canonical babbling to develop (Stark 1991). Auditory feedback may contribute to expanding the sounds of speech babies make.

One of the most significant milestones is reached at about 9 months when babies' communication becomes intentional. Infants make the critical discovery that they can use objects to have deliberate effects on other people and can use other people to have effects on objects (McLean 1990). Purposefully, babies send communicative signals—voice, gesture, eye gaze, and facial expressions—to accomplish their goals. According to Wetherby and Prizant (1993), babies intentionally communicate to have someone meet their needs and wants (behavior regulation) by requesting or protesting an object or action. For example, a baby with outstretched arms and eye gaze directed to an adult is requesting to be picked up and has a good chance of succeeding. A baby shaking his or her head "no" and pushing away a spoonful of spinach is clearly protesting. Babies communicate for social interaction by maintaining another's attention toward themselves. The "bye bye" or "blow a kiss" routines that can last for several minutes are examples of communicating for social interaction. Babies also communicate to direct the communicative partner's attention to the object or event that is the focus of interest (joint attention) as when showing an object or pointing to it while engaging someone's attention. During an episode of joint attention, a baby points to an object as a "What's that?" signal. Adults respond by providing a label for that object. This is often seen during book sharing. The baby points to a picture, and the adult offers "That's a duck." The baby points to a different picture and the adult obliges by offering "That's a bunny." The amount and quality of time during which a baby successfully engages in joint attention have been associated with vocabulary development (Warren and Yoder 1998). Successfully establishing joint attention enhances a child's ability to request information in later development (Yoshinaga-Itano and Stredler-Brown 1992). The nonverbal communication is eventually replaced by questions. A two-year-old can be relentless in asking "What's that?" questions. Joint attention and behavior regulation (specifically requesting) are the earliest functions of a baby's intentional communication, followed by requests for information. Successfully communicating these functions nonverbally is essential: it is a precursor to successful language development and use.

Nine months is an important age in terms of speech perception development. In English-speaking environments, babies demonstrate a preference for trochaic syllable patterns (a stressed syllable followed by an unstressed syllable, such as "mommy") rather than iambic syllables (a weak syllable followed by a strong one, such as "July") (Jusczyk, Cutler, and Rednaz 1993; Morgan 1995). This is relevant because the majority of content words in English are trochaic, or are made into trochaic words in child-directed speech; e.g., doggie, dolly, etc. By 9 months, babies have also acquired some knowledge about which sounds are allowed to go together in a sequence. English-speaking infants prefer to listen to consonant-vowel-consonant syllables that occur frequently, rather than consonant-vowel-consonant syllables that occur infrequently (Jusczyk, Charles-Luce, and Luce 1994). At this age, babies are thought to integrate rhythm preferences with their knowledge of speech sound sequences to segment words from speech (Morgan 1994).

Stage 5   From approximately 9 to 18 months, the baby's developing cognitive, social, and language skills become integrated with intentional communication and the beginning of meaningful speech (Stark, Bernstein, and Demorest 1993). Near the first birthday, strings of babble are replaced by single or paired consonant-vowel syllables that are more complex phonetically. Intonation becomes more complex, too, and a rising contour emerges. These short segments are paired with intentional communication. With time, the syllables become more word-like and eventually develop into true words.

First words generally emerge from the social and play routines between caretaker and baby (Snow, Dubher, and DeBlauw 1982) and are bound to the social context (Shannon 1998). First words are constructed from the child's repertoire of speech sounds, that is the consonant and vowel sounds the baby can produce (Stoel-Gammon 1998). In addition, babies select certain speech sounds from their repertoire that they seem to like to produce or can successfully produce and early words are based on that selection (Vihman 1998). Babies who have a larger repertoire of consonants are better prepared to produce more words (Stoel-Gammon 1998; Wilcox and Shannon 1998). During phonological development, the baby is thought to target whole-word shapes, rather than individual segments or phonemes (Viham 1998). Babies, therefore, need to be able to fully perceive the acoustics of speech and attend to it to develop spoken language as expected.

Toddlers continue to use jargon with more complex intonation until a knowledge of morphology (smallest meaningful sound units that can be a word or can be attached to words, such as /s/ for plurals or /d/ for past tense) and early grammar (Stark 1991) are acquired. A young child's vocal production and phonological system will continue to develop in a predictable sequence, with speech sound production becoming more refined over time. Even a child's pattern of errors is predictable and follows a developmental sequence. It is not until school age that all the sounds (of English) are represented in a child's speech.

Social Context for Communication

Play and Routines

The work of play   There must be interaction for communication to occur. Early mother-child interactions are characterized by elaborate, ritualized, and repetitive play and social routines (Snow, Dubber, and DeBlauw 1982). Through play, both adult and child share pleasurable and meaningful interactions while learning how to better communicate with each other. The earliest, preverbal social interactions and routines lay the foundation for the child's future verbal interactions and dialogues, while also serving the important function of having fun (Bruner 1983). Routines provide optimal opportunities for communication to develop and help teach the young child the rules of discourse: signaling, initiating, maintaining, and terminating the topic; taking turns; combining and ordering segments of language; and successfully communicating a range of language functions (Bruner 1974). Ritualized play almost guarantees contingency because the rules for turn taking are clearly established by the game itself. For example, in the game of "Peek-a-boo," the child's turn is signaled by the adult's covered eyes and anticipatory pause. The pause provides the opportunity for the baby to signal by voice or gesture. The baby signals for the adult's turn, and the smiling adult offers a contingent response, the predictable phrase "Peek a boo, I see you!" The baby quickly learns what to do to keep the game going and signals again. Adult and child take turns and even switch roles in terms of who initiates the game, once the routine has been learned. Rather than being the one who responds to "Peek a boo," the baby may later initiate the game by hiding under a blanket or covering his or her own eyes. The rules of this game are quite clear to baby and adult. There are specific signals and responses that make a game of "Peek a boo." Anything else will violate the game.

Such interactions are playful language-learning games or joint action routines that are highly predictable, repetitive, and, very importantly, reciprocal (Snow 1982). There are predictable openings, closings, and chances to continue the game. The child is provided ample opportunity to participate throughout the interaction and to experiment with producing different types of signals. As the child interprets the adult's communicative behaviors, so does the adult interpret and assign meaning to the child's attempts (McLean 1990; Snow 1976). These early interactions and "conversations" between caregiver and baby influence language acquisition and development (deVilliers and deVilliers 1979).

The Impact of Deafness

The System Crashes

When a baby is deaf, the system that normally allows communication and oral language to develop naturally goes awry. All the developmental processes and interactions previously described become fragile when a baby cannot hear. Deafness, de facto, limits a baby's speech perception experiences. The critical acoustic cues of child-directed speech that help babies segment the speech stream and learn the units of the native language are diminished, if not imperceptible. The ability to develop a phonological system is greatly compromised because of reduced experience of listening to caregivers and to the baby him or herself through auditory feedback. This has a ripple effect on a baby's ability to learn the lexicon (words) and syntax of the language environment.

Research into early vocal development has indicated that infants who are deaf often have restricted consonant repertoires as well as qualitative differences in their vowel production (Stoel-Gammon 1998). Other studies have indicated that babies who are deaf are delayed in producing canonical babble (Oller and Eilers 1988). This is significant when considering that a limited repertoire of consonants used in babble is associated with limited spoken word production (Stoel-Gammon 1998).

The transactional nature of parent-child communication is at risk when deafness renders both a parents' and child's signals difficult to read. A baby may not hear or respond to his or her mother's signals or behaviors, decreasing the mother's motivation to continue the interaction and causing her to feel ineffective (Dunst, Wortman Lowe, and Bartholomew 1990). In addition, factors such as a caregiver's psychological and emotional states and a baby's ability to engage in social interactions will likewise influence language development (Kuhl et al. 1998). Parents who are in emotional crisis because of the diagnosis of their child's deafness may not have the psychological energy to fully connect or communicate with their child (Koester and Meadow Orlans 1990; Schlessinger 1987.) Feelings of powerlessness and incompetence may influence early parent-child interaction negatively (Meadow Orlans, Bodner Johnson, and Sass-Leher 1996).

Important caregiver contributions to the language learning environment change or diminish frequently in hearing parent-deaf child communication. Hearing mothers' communication with their deaf babies has been characterized as more directive, intrusive, and controlling than that of hearing mothers with hearing children (Bodner-Johnson and Sass-Leher 1996). In a longitudinal study involving 40 prelingually deaf toddlers, Schlessinger (1987) found hearing mothers to be less flexible and more didactic in their interactions. Spencer and Gutfreund (1990) analyzed and compared the communicative behaviors of hearing mother-hearing baby and hearing mother-deaf baby dyads, as well as the communicative interactions across 4 dyads: hearing mother-hearing baby, hearing mother-deaf baby; deaf mother-deaf baby, and deaf mother-hearing baby. In the analyses, the hearing mothers with deaf infants were more directive in terms of topic and turn taking control, and subsequently offered less contingent responses. Schlessinger (1987) attributes this communicative style to a parent's sense of powerlessness over their child's deafness and feelings of loss of control. In an urgent attempt to regain control, parents may become over-zealous in their communication attempts. It is also possible that mothers (and caregivers) feel they have to control and direct the interaction in order to keep it going. Mothers will take their child's conversational turn when the child does not respond. The result is that caregiver communication with a deaf baby can become less supportive of language development. The basic tenets of following a child's lead, responding to the focus of a child's attention, and offering contingent responses are violated. The child and the adult become out of synch, causing the parent-child dialogue to become greatly distorted (Schlessinger 1987). Natural interactions that allow hearing children to develop communicative and social competence are derailed. The assumption that language will develop seamlessly no longer holds true in the presence of deafness. Instead, there are failed communication attempts resulting from the inability of parent and child to read or respond to each other's signals.

Poor dialogue and communicative defeat lead to timidity and passivity (Schlessinger 1987). Indeed, deaf children have been described as passive in their communication, not initiating and commenting upon a topic, not seeking out new information through questioning. Nicholas and Geers (1997) reported that their cohort of deaf, orally trained 36-month-old children communicated significantly less often than their hearing peers. Gaining their parents' attention and having their own needs met were the primary goals for communicating, whereas communication to gain information was extremely limited. Yoshinaga-Itano and Stredler-Brown (1992) concluded that clearly intended and readable nonverbal requests for information may be the skill that determines whether or not a child will develop age appropriate language skills. The babies in their study developed that skill very slowly, with a mean occurrence of less than once per half-hour video-taped session for 25- to-30-month-olds. The authors presented the possibility that the baby's communicative partner did not recognize the request for information and, thereby, extinguished the behavior in the young child. The implications go beyond language development. Schlessinger (1987) writes that the requesting and sharing of information between parent and child is a variable in the parent-child dialogue that influences emerging literacy.

In summary, deafness does not affect only the child; it affects the entire system of communication by adversely affecting: (a) adult sensitivity, responsivity, and contingency; (b) the belief in a child's communication capabilities; (c) the adult's fine-tuned language and infant-directed speech; and (d) the subsequent impoverishment of natural language-learning opportunities through typical routines. "The basic deprivation of profound congenital deafness is not the deprivation of sound; it is the deprivation of language " (Meadow 1980).

Traditional Approaches to Fix the System: Intervention

In a traditional model, a baby's hearing loss is diagnosed at a medical center or hearing and speech facility. An audiologist counsels the family about the impact of hearing loss on speech and language development, and may broach the subject of options in communication approaches. The audiologist then initiates the hearing aid process and refers the family to an early intervention program and/or a speech-language pathologist.

No matter how competent and compassionate the audiologist is, the family will leave the office feeling that somehow their child is broken and that they must find the right way to fix the problem. It has been our experience that the initial tendency is for parents to fixate on the implications that deafness has for speech development. At this point, parents may not understand the differences between speech and language. Parents may have gotten information about the critical period for language learning, which adds to the urgency of getting as much of the "right" speech therapy as soon as possible. Further confounding the heightened sense of stress are the families' own feelings of grief and loss.

Families enter programs or therapy looking to the professional to do something to help their baby learn to speak. Many therapists then begin "doing" therapy by referring to or following one of the many published curricula available. Speech therapy for deaf children historically has focused on targeting specific speech behaviors in an ordered, normative sequence. Therapeutic goals are comprised of specific speech segments, that is specific vowels, consonants, or syllables that may contrast or vary in suprasegmental or acoustic aspects. Therapy activities are constructed around eliciting those sounds. Daniel Ling's seminal work (1976) on the acoustics of English speech sounds and systematic approach to speech teaching for deaf children continues to be a primary model used in speech training programs.

Auditory training has been based on a hierarchy of skills and subskills (Erber 1982). The skills progress from the ability to detect, discriminate, identify, and comprehend auditory stimuli. There is also a prescribed sequence of the type of stimuli used, beginning with environmental sounds and progressing to speech sounds. Speech stimuli are presented in an orderly fashion from the discrete to the general: phoneme to syllable to word to phrase to sentence and finally connected discourse. Recent auditory training curricula for young children (Moog et al. 1995; Stout and Windle 1992; Vergara and Miskiel 1994) continue to be based on traditional models. Therapy activities are designed to have a child listen to the targeted stimuli and to demonstrate what are considered to be increasingly difficult auditory skills. The underlying hypothesis to this "bottom up" approach is that practice in detecting and then discriminating discrete phonemes or syllables in a structured therapy situation will result in those sounds transferring to spontaneous perception and spoken production, thereby facilitating oral language development.

An example of a therapy activity based on traditional models involves the use of animal noises as stimuli. The therapist may use toys for props to target specific speech sounds; a cow says "moo," a dog says "bow wow," the sheep says "baa" and the chick says "peep, peep, peep." The stimuli are chosen because of the vowel contrasts (/a/ /u/ /I/) and the early consonant contrasts (/p/ /b/ /m/), as well as suprasegmental aspects of duration (long vs. short), one syllable versus two syllables versus three syllables, and perhaps pitch (low for the cow and high for the chick). The animals parade along the table and both therapist and parent model the animal sounds for the child in repeated attempts to elicit the target. The therapist may then ask the child to demonstrate auditory discrimination of the animal sounds by choosing the appropriate prop in response to the spoken stimulus. A subsequent therapy session may have a similar format, but this time the animals may be used to demonstrate a change of rate (slow vs. fast). The activity and elicited/imitative tasks are modeled for the parents, who are then asked to follow through at home.

Although they provide useful theoretic information, models that target discrete hierarchical speech and listening skills need to be revised, particularly in work with infants. The models are incomplete and do not acknowledge the developmental sequences of communication and language development or the language environment:

1. There is limited acknowledgment of the transactional nature of communication between parent and child described earlier and the fact that early communication occurs and is learned within social contexts.

2. There is no provision for looking at how children use the targeted speech behaviors for different communicative meanings at various stages of development. Are they successfully using specific vocalizations to request or to establish joint attention?

3. The sequence of targeted subskills in these models does not account for the developmental sequences that babies go through as they learn to segment speech, derive meaning, formulate rules for language, and use those rules for linguistic expression. Babies who are deaf are expected to follow the same sequences of phonologic and spoken language development (at a delayed role) as do hearing children, yet they are currently taught to do so through systematic therapeutic experiences that do not follow normal sequences of perceptual development.

4. The traditional hierarchies are not consistent with the sequence of normal auditory perceptual development. Infants first listen to the whole of what is said, not to specific phonemes. It is through repeatedly listening to the speech stream, not segments, that they actively derive the rules of how sentences, phrases, words, and sounds are put together meaningfully. Current research in speech perception requires that we rethink the ways we go about auditory training. Often, in an attempt to have a child perceive or discriminate certain speech sounds, nonsense or monosyllables are used as stimuli. The efficacy of using syllables or monosyllabic words (e.g., "moo") for auditory training has been questioned. Hnath-Chisholm (1997) reported that speech perception training may be more effective if acoustically and linguistically complex utterances are used as stimuli. In this study, 4- to 8-year-old profoundly deaf children showed a greater improvement in perception of words that were differentiated by vowels when speech perception training was at the sentence level rather than at the isolated word level. Speech perception studies have suggested that infants figure out the distribution of phonemes and the rhythms of native speech through meaningful listening experiences. The importance of prosody in developing the rules of language has also been suggested. Practicing auditory discrimination of /bababa/ versus /moo/ may not be sufficient to help a child learn the emotional intent of a speaker (one of the earliest perceptual skills) nor does it help a child learn the boundaries between words and clauses. Cole (1992) writes that "isolated rote training or hypothetical auditory subskills is gen-

erally inappropriate and unnecessary with hearing impaired children under three years of age" (p. 109) and that "meaning in acoustic input is from gradual acquisition of spoken language . . . in the normal every day interacting and play with caregivers . . ." (p. 109).

5. Children actively discover the rules of a language system, not by imitation but through meaningful experiences, experimenting with the rules and by testing their own hypotheses.

6. Hierarchies of skills and subskills lead to intervention that is deficit based. The focus is on what the child cannot do and remediating it.

7. Traditional models which focus exclusively on audition and speech do not acknowledge the importance of visual and gestural components of prelinguistic development.

8. Traditional models of therapy may reinforce, rather than discourage, a directive style of communication between parent and child.

In order to address the goals targeted by the clinician, interactions and activities tend to be adult directed and initiated, rather than child initiated and adult responsive. Operationally, the child is expected to imitate the adult model. Parents who feel incompetent about their own skills and view the therapist as the expert, may adopt the clinician's more didactic communication style (I see this often, and can easily recognize which therapist a family is working with by the trademark way in which they talk to their child).

The therapist then, may be unknowingly contributing to a style of communication that detracts from an optimal language-learning environment.

A New Model for Intervention: Mediating the System

Deafness affects the family system as well as the system of communication. A family- centered model that takes a "top down" approach to communication development while incorporating certain traditional "bottom up" principles is suggested. The clinical challenge is to synthesize what is known about the developmental sequences of early communication and language, the transactional nature of successful adult-child communication, which salient acoustic cues in speech are available and meaningful, and how babies' speech perception and production develop. The goal is to develop effective and satisfying communication and interaction in which baby and adult continue to respond to and influence each other. Interaction is the context in which meaningful language, speech, and auditory experiences need to occur. That early connection between parent and baby is essential in a child's life and transcends all other issues arising from the diagnosis of deafness (e.g., speech therapy, cochlear implants, sign language). Developing therapy that encourages and respects parent-child connections requires that a clinician establish a program that (1) is family centered; (2) recognizes and helps shape parent/caretaker communicative influences; (3) is play based; and (4) is congruent with developmental sequences of infant communication and language, speech perception, and vocalization. The answer to parents' question "What do we do now?" is "Plenty." For families, babies, and certainly clinicians there is a tremendous amount of work to be done.

Family-Centered Intervention

The hallmark of family-centered programming is empowerment of families through developing competencies (Bodner-Johnson and Sass Leher 1996). Regardless of whether families choose an auditory oral or a sign route, they need to learn effective communicative strategies that accommodate their child's hearing loss. Helping parents to recognize, interpret, and respond appropriately to their baby's earliest signals will facilitate successful communication and language development. Positive successful communication promotes a sense of competence and builds esteem for both parent and child.

Parents who feel powerless or sense a lack of control appear to have difficulties providing optimal communication strategies for their children (Schlessinger 1987). Effective intervention must help them acknowledge their inherent ability to communicate with and care for their child, and so regain a sense of control in their lives (Bodner-Johnson and Sass-Lehrer 1996; Meadow-Orlans 1990; Roush 1994). The first order of intervention, then, is to help the family move from the crisis surrounding an unexpected diagnosis of deafness to a state of equilibrium. When parents are supported and viewed as competent, they can discover their strengths, learn what works for their child and their family, and make informed decisions (Moeller and Condon 1994).

So that they become confident of their skills in successfully communicating with their child, parents need to be actively involved in all levels of the programming, including assessments, goal setting, and therapy. They are respected as expert reporters and observers (Prizant and Wetherby 1993) and informed decision makers. The clinician is not a "fixer," but a coach: someone who teaches the rules of the game with strategies to win. Caregivers are the ones who take the ball and score the goal.

Families and children are heterogeneous and their rate of progress and development is highly variable. Consequently, there is an inherent process of ongoing assessment, refinement, and change. Parents are given time and support to make decisions about how to meet their child's unique needs and to change their minds when new information arises. Children are given time to show us how they respond to amplification and what seems to be their language-learning style.

A clinician working in a family-centered program needs a wide range of skills, often beyond that which is taught in training programs. What a clinician brings to the relationship with families—attitudes, biases, sensitivity, and role definitions/expectations— can have as significant an impact on the desired outcome as knowledge and clinical skill. To be effective, he or she must be willing to enter into a supportive, non-judgmental partnership with each family and accept their choices and decisions. By being objective and unbiased, professionals can help parents develop a sense of empowerment and self confidence (Roush 1994).

Caregiver Influences in Intervention

Families enter early intervention anticipating a program that is child focused. The perspective is that the baby is the one with the hearing loss and, therefore, needs special help. It is true that the baby is at great risk for significant language delays. A study by Lederberg and Everhart (1998) found that 3-year-old deaf preschoolers, who were identified early and enrolled in early intervention programs, had language similar to that of hearing 22-month-olds. The authors concluded that the focus of early intervention should be on improving the language-learning environment. Clinicians, then, need to coach parents on how to create that environment. This represents a significant paradigm shift: the parents are the focus and agents of intervention.

Adults shoulder much of the responsibility in successful adult-child communication and in supporting language development. Table II looks at adult contributions in hearing adult-hearing baby interactions and what impact deafness has on those interactions. Ways of encouraging successful adult-child communication are suggested. Parent education and guidance is aimed at helping caregivers consciously use communicative behaviors that are characteristic of an optimal language-learning environment, as described by Dunst et al. (1990). They are:

1. recognizing what draws and maintains a child's behavior,

2. interpreting a child's behaviors as intents to interact,

3. responding to the child's initiations in ways that encourage repeated child behavior and adult responsiveness,

4. encouraging child-initiated interactions rather than adult-directed ones, and

5. supporting and encouraging competence.

Recognizing a child's focus of attention   Feeling the urgency to help their baby develop speech, parents may lose sight of the significance of their baby's communicative signals and the need to recognize and reinforce them. Parents whose babies are deaf need to become sensitized to the baby's eye gaze and shifts because a

Table II Successful intervention approaches with babies who are deaf that address caregiver influences.

Communication with Hearing Babies	Communication with Deaf Babies	Intervention Approach	What Works
• Believe child capable of communication; • Interpret earliest signals as meaningful	• Parents' feelings impact belief • May not see baby's signals • Baby may signal less	• Educate; speech vs. language • Sensitize to eye gaze and shifts	• Face to face interaction • Social interaction routines
• Motherese (Intuitive)	• Child may not perceive acoustic features of motherese	• Teach appropriate auditory stimulation with routines • Provide visual information and tactile cuing for joint attention	• Amplify Intonation, Clear speech • Listening games based on routines
• Intuitive communication	• Conscious effort • Parents may feel incompetent	• Educate: the importance of play adaptive strategies	• Typical baby games; tickle and looming • Action routines
• Responsive and contingent communication	• Parent-directed • Less contingent	• Establish early turn taking • Follow child's lead	• Non-verbal games • Imitate baby • Wait!
• Fine-tuned language	• Ineffective communication; Simple language input	• Optimize prelinguistic skills • Teach strategies	• Play • Language within routines • Rephrase, model
• Countless opportunities	• Cumulative deprivation	• Family involvement • Consistent input	• Play, play, play

change may signal the baby's interests, attention, or topic of conversation (Koester and Meadow-Orlans 1990). As simplistic as this may sound, waiting for the child's signal and responding to it can be very difficult for some parents, given their tendency for directive communication. Nonetheless, following the child's lead is a valuable skill to reinforce because there is a positive causal relationship between mothers' behaviors that allow a child's attention to guide the interactive topics and the child's rate of language development (Spencer and Gutfreund 1990). Also, an interaction is more likely to continue when a child has initiated it and the parent responds to the child's interest.

When parents want to initiate a "conversation" with their baby, it is first necessary to get the child's attention. Hearing parents of deaf children often forget about effective, meaningful nonverbal communication (Schlessinger 1987). Because the exclusive use of audition for spoken language development is not possible for most hearing impaired children (Cole 1992), visual information and input for prelinguistic and linguistic communication is critical. This is true whether families choose an oral or total communication approach.

Much can be learned from deaf mothers' communication with their deaf babies. They use a range of nonverbal attention getting behaviors such as eye gaze, gestures, and facial expression, and physical strategies, such as physical contact or waving (Harris and Mohay 1997). These strategies are particularly important in the early stages of using amplification, when a child has had insufficient experience to extract meaning from the speech signals or to benefit from consistent use of appropriate amplification. Touching may get a baby's attention, whereas speech may not.

Interpreting a baby's behavior as intent to interact. Reading and interpreting a baby's earliest signal creates an upward spiral in the communication between parent and child. However, parents who are upset and grieving because of the deafness, who are focused on the implications for speech or "what is wrong" with their baby, may not be in tune with the infant's attempts at communication. In a study by Nienhuys, Horsborough, and Cross (1985) mothers' speech to deaf children was found to be less semantically contingent on the child's activity than mother's speech to hearing children. The authors suggested that the reduced contingency was a result of a mother's beliefs about the conversational competence of deaf children, rather than direct feedback from the child.

By observing parent-infant interaction, a clinician can interpret an infant's behaviors and signals for caregivers and comment upon what is "right" with the baby. Helping parents to recognize and be sensitive to the child's signals is the first step to re-establishing the belief that the baby is competent and capable of communicating. Increasing caregiver contingent responsiveness can then be facilitated. Caregivers need to provide the appropriate language scaffold based on what they think the baby is communicating— taking the baby's lead. The interpreting adult is a provider, expander, idealizer of utterances while interacting with the child—not a corrector or reinforcer (Bruner 1974).

Encouraging repeated child-initiated behavior and adult responsiveness Interactions that are child initiated rather than adult initiated are more likely to lead to a greater display of child competence (Dunst et al. 1990). This requires that caregivers be sensitive and responsive to the infant's signal, supporting the continuation of those behaviors. In a study by Spencer and Gutfreund (1990), timing differences of contingent responses were found between hearing mothers and deaf infants and deaf mothers and deaf infants. While hearing mothers were most likely to give a response while the baby was looking away, deaf mothers waited until their babies looked back before responding. The implications are significant. Hearing babies can get two forms of input simultaneously; visually by looking at an object and auditorily by hearing caregivers' speech about the object. This is not the case for deaf infants, who when looking away, may not receive the auditorily presented information. The deaf mothers increased the opportunities for their deaf children to receive language input by waiting to respond. Deaf babies of hearing parents receive less linguistic input, even when their caregivers expose them to it. Coordination between adult communication and deaf children's visual attention then is important for language input.

Even as their babies become preschoolers, hearing parents with deaf children continue to have difficulty coordinating their communication with the child's visual attention. This is compounded by the fact that deaf children may not attend to all the visual information provided by their caregivers. In a comparative study of communication between hearing parents/hearing preschoolers and hearing parents/deaf preschoolers, Lederberg and Everhart (1998) found that at age 22 months, deaf children saw less that half of their mothers' utterances and that at 3 years, they did not see 25% of the mothers' communication. Because the amount of contingent language a child receives is critical for language development, caregivers need to learn the sequential timing used by deaf mothers (Spencer and Gutfreund 1990). This is true whether parents are signing or not.

Supporting and encouraging competence Caregivers fine tune their language to young children to reflect and support the child's developing communication abilities (McLean 1990). The fine tuning is a way of modeling language that is expected to develop next. In this way, parents help stretch their child's communication development and competence.

This can be a more difficult task for caregivers whose babies are deaf. The caregivers' language input can remain "stuck" at a simple stage, either because they have not developed more advanced communication strategies themselves or because the child is not effectively signaling their readiness to move ahead. Teaching caregivers the sequential stages of language development, to fine tune their language, and to develop more sophisticated skills is a necessary and primary component of intervention. Yoshinaga-Itano and Stredler-Brown (1992) suggested that the deaf babies in their study developed the skill of requesting information slowly because adults were not providing the necessary scaffold. Whereas hearing caregivers with hearing infants interpreted their babies' pointing fingers as "What's that?"—an early request for information—hearing caregivers with deaf infants responded to the pointed fingers as a requests for objects ("Give me that") or actions ("Make it move"). The adults interpreted their deaf babies' signals as one of an earlier stage and therefore did not provide the appropriate language model for the next step. The authors cite the need for professionals to provide parents with techniques that will facilitate the development of a young child's competence to ask questions to acquire information. Lederberg and Everhart (1998) found that mothers of deaf preschoolers used language less and gestures more when communicating with their children than hearing mothers did with their hearing preschoolers. Again, the adults did not provide the appropriate language model for the child. Consequently, their children vocalized and gestured, but for nonlinguistic purposes. The children did not move into using language as did their hearing peers; only 38% of the utterances produced by the deaf 3-year-old subjects contained language.

The combined effect of reduced language received by the child, reduced use of language (not communication) used by the communicative partner, or a simpler form of language model is an environment that does not support language learning. A primary goal for early intervention is to teach parents specific strategies for creating a language-learning environment. In such an environment, parents can support infants' communicative competence, and can coordinate visual communication-attention, contingent responsiveness, and appropriate language scaffolds. The social and joint action routines that occur naturally and repeatedly between caregiver and child support such a language- learning environment (Snow 1977: Bruner 1974 ; Ninio and Bruner 1976) and should be capitalized upon in creating programs of early intervention. Such routines and their use are further described in the sections The Work of Play and Putting It All Together.

Infant Capacities and Development in Intervention

Intervention techniques and goals need to be appropriate to the child's level of development and so should match a child's maturational capabilities (Wilcox and Shannon 1998). A system for nonverbal, prelinguistic communication develops before a verbal system (Wilcox and Shannon 1998). Babies use gestures, facial expressions, and voice to communicate before they use words. Their communication is nonintentional before it is intentional. Babies develop vowel sounds before consonants, and continue to develop speech sounds as their neuro-muscular control develops. Babies cannot "voice on demand" until they are cognitively and physically ready (Ling 1976). Babies appear to use prosody to derive early meaning for spoken language (Bloom 1974). Babies' early communication and words are first bound to the social context and understood in that context (Warren and Yoder 1998).

Each contributing constituent of infant communication has its own set of developmental sequences. It is insufficient to target only one domain, such as speech or auditory perception to the exclusion of the entire system of infant communication development. Planning appropriate intervention requires integrating the developmental sequences across all domains into meaningful interaction.

Speech perception

Amplify The rationale for fitting infants with amplification as soon as possible is obvious. The goal is to minimize the disruption of auditory input and to thereby minimize the consequent delays in spoken language development. Certainly one of the first and most important steps in intervention is providing the baby with appropriate amplification as early as possible. The next step is to educate parents about the importance of early auditory input and the need to have the baby wear aids consistently. Getting into the habit of putting hearing aids on very young infants has significant practical advantages: the babies do not have the motor control to pull them off. Parents who establish that hearing aids are a part of the infant's routine, like diaper changing and feeding, may be able to avoid the "battle of the wills" that can develop later. Older babies often refuse to keep their socks on, let alone hearing aids. Early amplification does have its problems. Feedback is almost inevitable, given powerful amplification, small ear canals, and the fact that babies spend a lot time in positions where feedback is likely to occur. The acoustical problems take patience, and usually several sets of earmolds to correct. As for the baby who tugs and removes the hearing aids, there are behavioral techniques that can be useful. Providing enjoyable distraction such as children's television programs and videos like Sesame Street or Barney is one approach. Pairing the auditory input with a positive reinforcer, such as face-to-face interaction with a smiling adult helps set the stage. Timing is also an important factor to consider. A baby who is tired or otherwise cranky is less likely to keep on the hearing aids; however, parents need to learn to be firm in letting the child know that keeping the hearing aids on is non-negotiable. If spoken language development is a priority for the parents, the baby needs to have as much auditory experience as possible.

Auditory training The focus of auditory training must integrate what is known about developmental sequences in infant speech perception with meaningful language interactions because:

• Children respond to intonation before they respond to specific phonetic forms (Bloom 1974)

• Children's earliest response to speech is largely affective and connotational (Bloom 1974).

• Babies link the emotional intent of the prosodic cues they hear with the context. The ability to discriminate sounds involves different capacities than the ability to associate sounds with words (Bloom 1974).

• The ability to relate a sound stimulus to the existence of a sound making object does not appear until age 8 to10 months (Menyuk 1974).

• Infants behave differently to speech versus non-speech stimuli. Speech stimuli elicit a greater amount of infant vocalization than nonspeech stimuli (Menyuk 1974).

• Studies suggest that infants first listen to suprasegmental features, then familiar word length utterances later on, at around the time of the transition from babbling to words (Menyuk 1974).

• Studies suggest that babies use prosodic cues to help them segment the speech stream into meaningful units (Morgan 1996; Morgan and Saffran 1995; Jusczyk, Cutler, and Rednaz 1993; Jusczyk, Luce, and Charles-Luce 1994)

The notion of initiating auditory training for very young infants with activities based on environmental sounds, segmental (different speech sounds) or single word stimuli (as is done in common clinical practice) is incongruent with what is known about normal infant speech perception. Having infants first listen to drums or cowbells and relating the sounds to their sources is developmentally inappropriate. Auditory training models that purport to acknowledge and address the primacy of the development of suprasegmental perceptual skills do not take into account that babies first listen for the emotional intent behind what is being said to them. Activities like discriminating /moo/ from /peep, peep, peep/ (described earlier), although accurately targeting differences in suprasegmental cues of rate, duration, and intensity do little to provide the infant with information about whether or not the speaker was angry or friendly, familiar or unfamiliar. Nor does that approach help infants learn to segment the speech stream by discovering the acoustic cues for word or phrase boundaries. A segment cannot be segmented.

Listening experiences need to be created that are consistent with the ways infants develop communicatively and the ways adults interact with infants. Auditory training must be linked with language development. Rather than drums and cowbells, animal sounds, monosyllabic words, or nonsense syllables, stimuli that exploit the wealth of prosodic information in child-directed speech is recommended. Rather than contrived activities, typical parent-child interactions and routines known to support language acquisition provide the milieu. Auditory training can occur every time parent and child interact if conscious use of child-directed speech is integrated into daily routines and play. Auditory training becomes re-integrated into the system, rather than being an isolated variable and event. When "auditory training" is demystified and put into the context of parent-child interaction, caregivers take primary responsibility and develop competency. Specific examples appear in the section Putting It All Together.

Speech Production

Hearing parents are focused on speech. Even those families who are involved in total communication programs or who have taken sign classes, predominantly communicate with their child through speech (Lederberg and Everhart 1998).

Ling (1976) makes particularly relevant points about teaching speech to young deaf children that must be emphatically reiterated in this age of early identification and intervention:

• No attempt to teach specific speech sounds should be made until a variety of pleasant vocal patterns is habitually used for communication and in vocal play (p. 114).

• Systematic training for speech development based on normal acquisition of phonology is appropriate for infants who are 7 months or older (p. 112).

• The most appropriate way to encourage vocal production is through "social conditioning." Live voice from the person in contact with the child is most effective (p. 198).

• Vocalization should be reinforced with natural language—not simply the vowel sounds elicited from the child (p. 198).

• One cannot demand vocalization until it can be produced spontaneously (p. 198).

• Provoking laughter by tickling and physical play, encourages vocalization (p. 198).

Because of parents' wishes, it is tempting to launch into a speech training program. Yet, as Ling describes, it is inappropriate to focus on specific speech sound production in infancy. What is appropriate is to encourage "vocalization." The question is how? The stages of early infant communication provide useful answers (see table I). Very young infants vocalize more in face-to-face interactions with a responsive adult or when stimulated visually. They vocalize in response to appropriate child-directed speech. As babies become more physically active, they vocalize more when engaged in sensorimotor activity. Parents and clinicians then can take advantage of these stages of play and social interactions to increase an infant's rate of vocalization. However, eliciting speech must also occur within interactions that are linked to and facilitate language development. Speech is insufficient unto itself. Stimulating and encouraging speech production for prelinguistic and linguistic purposes can be accomplished through naturally occurring social language and joint action routines and play.

Social Interactive Context in Intervention: The Work of Play

One of the sometimes unexpected challenges clinicians face is teaching parents to understand and accept how very important play is in facilitating communication development and language acquisition. Parents who have come through a medical system armed with advanced technologies (ABR, CT scans, digital hearing aids, cochlear implants, etc.) often anticipate therapy to be equally mysterious or technical. How surprising it must be to go to therapy to play, and to accept that blowing bubbles or knocking down blocks is, in fact, the work of caregivers and babies.

Playful, ritualized social and language routines that both parent and child enjoy provide the setting for the earliest intervention. Play also serves the very important function of enjoyment for baby and parent. Once a parent discovers which games and routines work with the baby, the parent will use them over and over again, finding success in establishing communication. Play routines help parents to recognize their strengths while encouraging them to replace a directive style of communication with one that supports language development. Preserving adult responsivity, sensitivity, and contingency is critical.

Ritualized, preformatted language routines (e.g., "Peek a boo, I see you") have an important role in parent-child interaction. Hearing parents are given a heightened sense of successfully communicating with their deaf baby because the chances of failure are diminished. Preformatted routines narrow the options of what the parent and child have to say to continue the interaction. The rules of the game (when is it time to take a turn, what is the required response) are predetermined and predictable, so that interpreting communicative behaviors is easier. The routines also provide countless opportunities to give repeated and consistent language input, relevant and acoustically salient speech input, and listening experiences that are meaningful and support language acquisition.

In an analysis of mother-child interactions, Snow (1977) reported that mothers and their babies played such formatted games twice per hour by age 3 months and four times per hour by 6 months. By 6 months, then, the baby had experienced these interactions 1000 times. How much more powerful than going to therapy one or two hours per week!

Clinicians need to survey parents for what they know their baby enjoys. Is there a special tickle game they play or a special bath time routine? Is there a favorite toy? The parents' input is needed to adapt and reinforce a routine that incorporates what the family may already be doing and enjoying at home. It also helps parents realize how much they are already communicating with their child.

How are these language routines constructed and initiated? There are two parts to the routine. First, an action needs to be clearly seen by the child, because it is easy to understand and captures the young child's interest. Second is the language that accompanies the action.

Once the child understands the fundamental aspects of the actions and can predict what will happen, the child can focus on the language and begin to understand it. This occurs even in the earliest simplest routines. Tickling and looming games are typical of adult-baby interactions that are routinized. "Gonna getcha" is played by the adult creeping a hand slowly and rhythmically up the baby's leg, coordinated with the repetitive phrase. The adult's pitch rises as the hand reaches the baby's torso. The adult pauses, then tickles the baby's stomach while expressing "Gotcha!" more loudly and with stress on the first syllable. The baby laughs and the cycle is repeated. After a time, the baby learns to anticipate the tickle from the visual, auditory, and tactile cues of the game. There is a back and forth exchange between parent and child. The baby knows when to take a turn and has an active role in continuing the routine. Parent and child are successfully reading each other's signals and enjoying the interaction. As simple as this game may seem, it is indeed "therapy."

Caregiving routines, such as bathing, changing diapers, and feeding can be made routine. The baby learns that a specific gesture, facial expression, and language predict an event. The caregiver's "P U" accompanied by the usual gesture and facial expression can only mean one thing!

The auditory stimuli used repetitively in the routines must be audible and meaningful, since there must be meaning attached to a recent auditory event for the young child to develop listening skills (Cole 1992). One of the clinician's responsibilities then is to determine the auditory stimulus to be used to gain and maintain attention and to differentiate the routines. Which spoken auditory stimuli make acoustic sense? This is where Ling's work is invaluable. Suprasegmental cues of duration, intensity, and pitch can often be audible to profoundly deaf children who have appropriate amplification. Profoundly deaf children, who had difficulty discriminating speech segments were able to discriminate rising intonational contours from falling contours at a level better than chance (Engen, Engen, and Clarkson 1983). Vowels (/a/, /u/, /i/) that have acoustic energy that is available to profoundly deaf children who wear aids, as well as "Step 1" consonants /p, b/ /m/ /w/ /h,f,v/ (Ling 1976) need to be included in the spoken language of the routine. This is not a difficult task, since the language associated with many "baby games" already uses those phonemes, e.g., "Peek-a-boo," "Wee, wee, wee" in This Little Piggy," "Who's belly?" and "Bye bye." The auditory stimuli can change as do the routines. However, they should be based on the acoustic and developmental principles established by Ling (1976) and should always be embedded in language. This will ensure that the baby has a systematic exposure to salient cues for speech while the primacy for language-learning opportunities is maintained.

For example, hand clapping games are typical games for babies and parents. "Pat-a-cake" is a social routine that provides a rich auditory experience, visual and tactile cues, as well as opportunity for joint attention, turn taking, contingent responsiveness, and predictable language sequences. The game begins with a repeated refrain, "Pat-a-cake," with stress on the first syllable. The third line "Baker's man'" has the same number of syllables but the rhythm and stress are different. Stress and syllable patterns change in a repetitive way and are reinforced through the rhythm of clapping. At the phoneme level "pa-ta-cake" targets point consonants /p,t,k/ paired with vowels.

As children move into intentional communication and are beginning to express early language meanings, the routines change again. Babies have topics that they like to talk about, such as things that disappear, stop, or change. "All gone" or "Uh oh" are phrases that are acoustically salient because of their prosody and phonetic structure and are readily incorporated into the game. Blowing bubbles is a wonderful and enjoyable routine. Parents bring out the bubbles, much to every baby's delight. The baby signals excitement through voice and facial expression, and perhaps signals wanting them by looking at the jar and then the adult, or pointing and vocalizing. The adult responds contingently "Bubbles? You want bubbles?" and blows. The adult then proceeds to "Pop, pop, pop" (acoustically appropriate phrase for marking a change of state). The baby seeing that they have disappeared looks to the adult who then says "Uh oh...all gone." The baby signals to the adult for more, and the cycle repeats. This routine provides a repeated, predictable language context within a parent-child interaction that is linguistically and auditorily appropriate. The baby has the opportunity to take a turn, hear/see the label for the requested object and action, and to request it again. The adult provides a preformatted script and appropriate contingent language that will be repeated every time the bubbles are brought out. Again, play is therapy.

Social or joint action routines can be created around anything that holds the baby's attention. Parents naturally play these games with babies, but in the case of deaf children the communication connected with the interaction needs to be carefully and consciously constructed. Although parents may at first feel self-conscious or insecure with their ability to do this, with time the behaviors become automatic and natural, allowing parent and child to gain confidence in their communication skills (Koester and Meadow-Orlans 1990).

Putting it All Together

Table III presents a guideline for using parent-infant interactions and routines as the milieu for intervention that supports communication, language, and speech perception and production development. The table is an adaptation and synthesis of tables I and II and follows the sequences and stages of infant communicative development. The routines/interactions are illustrative, not prescriptive or definitive. Clinicians are encouraged to create others that are individualized for the families they serve and that are appropriate to the developmental stage of the infant. The table presumes that babies identified in the newborn period will endure little lag time before amplification and intervention are initiated.

Stage I. Phonation/Reflexive sound making

The baby's sounds are reflexive and noncommunicative, yet the caregivers respond as if they were. Caregivers speech with very young infants is rich in prosody and phonetically simple. A baby who already has appropriate amplification will begin to have meaningful listening experiences and may be able to perceive prosodic cues. The baby cries, the caregiver responds in a repeated way that eventually the baby will come to predict. The baby will learn to recognize and draw meaning from the adult's speech. Crying followed by an adult response will occur many times per day over the course of these early months, reinforcing the meaning of the adult's speech as comforting.

Table III Intervention that integrates developmental sequences and stages of vocal speech perception and communicative development; adult contribution and social/joint action routines. Stages of development as presented are general and suggested, not definitive.

Vocal Development/	Routine Interaction	Caretaker Contribution	Auditory Stimuli
Stage 1: Phonation/Reflexive Sound making (vegetative sounds)	• Caregiving • Feeding/diapering • "Rocking" o–"goodnight" routines	• Interpret signals as meaningful • Language scaffold related to state • Emotive child-directed speech • Sensitize to eye gaze shifts	• Amplify "Who's hungry?" "You OK?" "Whose hiccups?" "Sooo ... Sleepy!" (Rising intonation)
Stage 2: Cooing/Reactive Sound Making (Vowel-like sounds, /k,g/)	• Face to face (person-person orientation) • Looming, tickle games • Making faces • Visual stimul	• Establish shared attention, • Encourage turntaking continued exchanges • Child-directed speech • Contextual language information/attention	• Amplify contingent imitation "Coooh, so pretty!" "Mommy's keys" (Intonation, vowel stress, increased vowel duration within clause)

Table III continued

Vocal Development/	Routine Interaction	Caretaker Contribution	Auditory Stimuli
Stage 3: Exploratory sounds/ Activity Sound Making (raspberries, squeals, clicks, laughter)	• Peek a boo! • So big! • Back and forth (in swing) • Bouncing, kicking • Play with objects	• Establish joint attention • Supplement vocalization with temporally patterned visual, tactile, kinesthetic and vestibular stimuli • Interpret apparent intent • Encourage extended turn taking	• Amplify • Routinized language • Increased vowel duration stress, pause within clause
Stage 4: Canonical Babbling/ Activity Sound Making /dadada, mamama/ variegated /dadi/	• Pattycake, finger plays • Social routines (Bye, bye: blow kiss) • Pop beads, pop up toys • Play with objects, actions • Physical play; bouncing •	• Follow child's lead • Encourage joint attention, turntaking, babbling • Supplement vocalization with temporally patterned visual, tactile, kinesthetic and vestibular stimuli • Respond contingently • Encourage babbling	• Amplify • Ritualized language • Varying stress and rhythm "Bye bye Big Bird!" "All gone!" "Pop pop pop!" (bubbles) Baby forms /doggie/

Table III *continued*

Vocal Development/	Routine Interaction	Caretaker Contribution	Auditory Stimuli

Stage 5:
Communicative Sound Making
Prelinguistic Intentional
communication
(Requesting commenting)
	Book reading
	Simple nursery rhymes
	"Where's your belly?"
	"Where's your nose?"
		• Follow child's lead
		• Label the object of focus
		• Map intentional, nonverbal signs!
		• Fine-tune language
		• Contingent responses
		• Coordinated visual
		  communication-attention
		• Encourage increased rate of
		  communication
			Amplify
			"Look! What's that?
			It's a …"
			"More? Again?
			That's a …"
			(in response to
			indexical point)
			Rhythm, melody

Stage 6:
First words
Intentional communication
Early meanings of first words
	"What's that?"
	Context-bound
	Coordinated person-object
	orientation
		• Follow child's lead
		• Semantic and contextual
		  contingency
		• Rephrase, expand child's
		  utterance
			Amplify
			"Uh oh, fall down!"
			"It broke!"
			"Hooray"
			"No, no, no!"

Stage 2. Cooing/reactive sound making

The baby begins to have more volitional control of vocalization and physical movement. The baby produces a sound and the caregiver readily engages in an imitative conversation. The adult's response encourages the baby to make the sounds again in this face-to-face social interaction. Beginning dialogue skills are being established as caregiver and child go back and forth, taking turns and imitating each other. Again, the adult's speech is rich in intonation and provides prosodic information that may be available to the infant who has received appropriate amplification.

Because babies also vocalize in response to visual stimuli, mirrors in cribs and turning, visible mobiles are particularly useful. The adult "scripts" the focus of the baby's attention with simple phrases or sentences that contain a great many prosodic cues (rise/fall intonation, pause, stressed word, etc.) and low frequency-loaded phonemes. "Oooooh, there's the bunny!" or "Who's that? Who's that baby? You!"

Caregivers need to overlay language onto the baby's vocalization and provide the language model for the focus of attention. Consistent with child-directed speech, the adult's speech should be accompanied by animated facial expression and gesture. The adult pauses, acoustically marking the baby's turn. The baby responds and the routine recycles. This simple back and forth dialogue that accompanies face-to-face interaction or visual stimuli can be derived from anything that holds the baby's interest; an adult's funny face, keys, a shiny watch, etc.

Stage 3. Exploratory sounds/activity making sounds

During this time, babies make all sorts of funny sounds as they explore what they can produce. A primary goal is for the baby to receive auditory feedback through appropriate amplification that will encourage the continuation of the noisemaking. Caretakers begin games of "peek a boo" or "so big" by acting upon the child. The baby laughs, the adult interprets it as a signal to continue and the cycle repeats. "Peek a boo" is a wonderful acoustic stimuli with many salient cues; vowels, stress, pause. The enjoyable routine is repeated until baby or adult have had enough. The routine, with its predictable, preformatted language and rules will be repeated endless times throughout the weeks and months of a young child's life. Caregiver and child have a shared focus of attention (the action of the game) and there is opportunity for maintaining turn taking, and thereby increasing the rate of the child's communication.

Stage 4. Canonical babbling/Activity sound making

Canonical babbling emerges at about the time babies begin to be able to explore their environment. Having toys and objects that babies can move and mouth, or providing opportunities to be active will result in increased vocalization. This stage is critical in that babies begin to expand their production into syllables with more adult-like timing. This is the point where deaf babies begin to sound different from their hearing peers, and where delays in phonological development can begin to occur. Amplification is critical to help the child develop auditory feedback. Repetitive sounds can be patterned through other modalities in conjunction with speech, such as bouncing the baby on the adult's knees while accompanying the action with a rhythmic chant, "Bounce, bounce, bounce." "Oops" provides an unexpected refrain as the baby is allowed to slide down between the adult's legs. The game is rhythmical, prosodic, and fun. Providing opportunities for the baby to hear speech with adult timing within a social context may help the baby develop canonical syllables. Parents may have their own version of action games. One family I worked with played "zoop" with their infant. The father "zooped" her to the right, then "zooped" her to the left, and finally "zooped" her overhead. The chant accompanied the rhythm of the movement. Adults can do much to elicit canonical syllables by using diminutive forms for words: doggie, nai nai (night night), binky (pacifier). Social routines, like "bye bye" often include canonical syllables as well. Creating a social routine that uses canonical syllables provides repeated opportunity for auditory input and for the baby to produce those sounds to initiate or continue the interaction.

Stage 5. Communicative Sound Making/Intentional Communication

As babies become intentional they use a number of means to express themselves purposefully. They reach, they show an object, they point, and they use voice and eye gaze to have their needs met and to engage in joint attention. Deaf babies can stay in a prelinguistic stage for an extended time, as evidenced by the well-documented delays in language acquisition in deaf preschoolers. Book reading routines can be an effective way for babies to learn a lexicon and to move into language. Ninio and Bruner (1976) describe the action scheme used in book reading routines with babies. The adult says "Look!" to gain the baby's attention and then asks "What's that?" while pointing to a picture on a page. The baby may point, vocalize, or gesture. The adult accepts any signal and then labels the picture. The adult's utterances are limited and form the "rules" for reading the book. Every time baby and adult read a book together, the adult will use the same format. "Look! What's that? It's a . . ." Initially, the adult may take all the conversational turns. The baby learns through the repeated and consistent format when it's his or her time for a turn in the conversation and that a response is in fact expected. If the baby is interested in the picture, the adult will repeat the label, stressing the word. The baby may vocalize, and the babbled response will be treated as if it were a word. Through repeated book sharing routines, the baby's gestures and vocalizations are interpreted as referential. Babbled utterances will be reinforced until the syllable does in fact come to be recognized as referring to the object. Book sharing routines then are powerful interactions. Adults present a closed set of repeated utterances that differ in prosody; a vocative, a question, and a declarative statement with stress on the end. The label is offset by a pause, and because it is stressed, the word will have greater intensity. And because the baby is most likely seated on the caregiver's lap, the distance between the adult's mouth and microphone of the hearing aid (assuming ear level amplification) is almost ideal for optimal auditory input. The baby is exposed to these repeated acoustic cues within a joint activity that has clear visual support (the pictures in the book) and that is enjoyable. The baby's vocalization and gesture are reinforced by the adult, and may be shaped into a word.

Stage 6. First words

As babies first acquire words, they communicate for a variety of purposes. For example "cookie" can mean, "I want a cookie" "The cookie is all gone" "The cookie fell" or "There's the cookie." Recognizing what babies first talk about and then providing the appropriate language scaffold within a routine helps lead the way to the next stage of language development. A shared action routine of building up blocks and knocking them down is a typical routine that older babies enjoy and will stay engaged with for many cycles. An adult begins to build a block tower, with the appropriate language. "Let's build. Build it up." Each stacked block is accompanied by "Oooh, it's big. Up, up, up. Here's more!" The excitement builds until the blocks tumble. "Hooray!" marks the completion of the construction. "Look!" Adult and child knock it down. "Uh oh! They fell down! Boom! Do it again?" The baby laughs, looks to the adults, and hands over a block. Adult and child begin to build the faulty tower again. The baby anticipates the fall, produces "Uh oh" when the blocks crash and requests the routine again. The rules of the game and the accompanying language are clear and repeated along each step of the action. The script includes language for success (hooray), recurrence (do it again? more?), movement (fall down), and notice (look). This typical play routine provides opportunities for the baby to use the language he or she already has, while providing models for the next step of development. There is movement and excitement that encourages vocalization, and relevant linguistic input that is auditorily salient. As the routine is repeated and the child learns the format, he or she may take on the role of chief engineer. The adult initially accepts any language the child produces, but eventually ups the ante for a more sophisticated response. The baby learns the meanings of the language he experiences repeatedly within the context and is likely to produce language within that context.

Summary

Research, technology, and professional drive have made the identification of hearing loss in infants a reality. Although there has also been significant forward movement toward the provision of optimal amplification through advanced technology and fitting paradigms, clinical research that specifically addresses the development of communication, language, and speech production and perception in infants who are deaf is lacking. Nonetheless, babies who are deaf are being identified at birth and we have a professional and ethical responsibility to rethink the nature of efficacious intervention.

Current clinical practice continues to be based upon traditional "bottom up" models for speech and auditory training that are incongruous with what is thus far known about normal infant speech perception, production, and language development. Such practice may result from a skewed focus on the infant's communicative production and the perspective that language must be taught rather than actively and systematically acquired by the child. The efficacy of such intervention is questioned, since studies continue to indicate that deaf children are at great risk for significant delays in language development (Lederberg and Everhart 1998). Those delays have implications for literacy development as well.

A systems model that addresses the need to create a supportive language-learning environment through the integration of adult contributions, stages and sequences of infant communicative development, the transactional nature of communication, and the social/interactive context is presented. The model is family focused and places the parent- child connection at the center of therapy. Meaningful social interactions and routines replace traditional, contrived therapeutic activities that target discrete speech and auditory goals outside of a linguistic and social context. By using ritualized language routines and play as the vehicle for intervention, we encourage the development of the growing child's ability to have meaningful experiences that support speech production and perceptual development, to use language for discourse, and to comment upon or gain information about the world. Through language routines, parents develop adaptive strategies that nurture successful communication with their child which enhances the parent-child relationship.

Intervention must consider the following:

• Parents are the focus. Although it is the baby who is deaf, it is the caregivers who need to learn adaptive strategies that facilitate communication development. Many of the intuitive, unconscious behaviors hearing parents use in communicating with their hearing infants need to be used more consciously and deliberately by parents of deaf babies. Through teaching adaptive strategies and supporting parent-child interactions, clinicians encourage sensitivity, responsivity, and contingency.

• Clinicians are coaches who cannot "fix" the babies and families they work with. They can educate caregivers about effective strategies and developmental sequences, while providing support and information. Caregivers have ultimate responsibility for their baby, and consequently should be the ones "doing" therapy. Families are thereby supported in regaining their sense of competence.

• Babies acquire language. They are active learners, not passive recipients. Early parent-infant routines, through preformatted and repeated experiences, are powerful experiences for children acquiring language. Social routines also provide a meaningful context for the development of auditory and speech skills. Clinicians support the use of such routines and help determine what is the appropriate language and auditory stimuli to be used during those interactions.

- Babies move through predictable stages. Intervention must be appropriate to a baby's stage of development, across all domains.

- Infants use prosodic cues to learn to segment speech into meaningful units in an apparently sequential way, listening first to the "whole" of the prosodic contour before individual segments. They first listen to the emotional intent of the speech directed to them and use prosody to help crack the linguistic code. Early auditory training therefore should exploit the richness of child-directed speech, rather than using nonmeaningful segments.

- The initial stages of intervention are about input, not production. As Ling (1976) points out, targeting specific speech sounds before a baby is seven months old or is spontaneously vocalizing is developmentally inappropriate. The initial focus should be to help caregivers develop their skill at creating a language-learning environment through the pleasure and enjoyment of connecting with their child. Preserving that connection transcends all.

The author gratefully acknowledges friends and mentors who influenced her work and shaped the thought behind this chapter: David Luterman, Deborah Topol, Mary Jane Johnson, and Laura Knox.

CHAPTER 5

Assistive Hearing Technologies

Richard C. Seewald

My work with hearing impaired children began in the early 1970s. The decisions I had to make at that time regarding which technology to apply were relatively straightforward. Would I fit body-worn or ear level instruments? Would I fit one ear or two? These decisions were made primarily on the basis of the child's age and the presumed degree of hearing loss in each ear. Infants (the few I saw) and toddlers with severe to profound hearing loss all received body-worn instruments. Possibly the most difficult decision I faced was in choosing among three button-type receivers (wideband / low output; narrow-band / high output; and something in between called "standard" or "normal"). Fortunately, no one ever asked me to describe the scientific principles upon which my choice was based. At that time a complete analysis of hearing aid performance consisted of speaking into the aid, at a reduced volume control wheel setting, and making a judgement about the quality of amplified sound. We did not have an electroacoustic analysis system to measure performance directly. Finally an aided audiogram would be obtained to document benefit from amplification—and that was that.

Some of the children I fitted during those early years benefited greatly from use of their hearing aids. Some of the children benefited somewhat and some did not appear to benefit at all. I had always suspected that some in the latter group wore their hearing aids only when they came to see me for their annual evaluation—hearing aids in mint condition were easy to spot. However, some in the latter group did not pretend. They had discontinued their use of hearing aids for lack of any self-perceived benefit and boldly told me so. There was nothing else to offer from the "Technology Department"—it was either hearing aids or no hearing aids. The complete range of assistive technology options had been explored.

By the mid-1970s, FM auditory trainers had become available—large body-worn units with yet another set of button-type receivers. These systems were viewed more as educational devices than as personal amplification systems. Consequently, audiologists rarely participated directly in the selection and fitting process, such as it was. In the location at which I was working, FM auditory trainers were fitted by the manufacturer's representative. The approach to selection and fitting of FM auditory trainers employed by these individuals can best be described as "one size fits all."

I recall one child in particular. I had fitted the child with an ear level hearing aid on her right ear only. She had a severe sensorineural hearing loss in the right ear with no measurable hearing in the left. During one visit to the clinic, the mother announced that her child was now wearing an auditory trainer at school. Further enquiry revealed that the FM auditory trainer had been fitted by the manufacturer's representative to the child's left ear. Reportedly the advantage of this creative arrangement was that the child could wear both her own hearing aid and the FM auditory trainer simultaneously. No doubt, this representative had visions of himself with the Nobel Prize in hand! Unfortunately, the FM auditory trainer that was fitted to this child's "dead ear" was nothing more than an expensive illusion, as it often was in those days.

In view of the relative complexity of modern technology, the point of this story may be as relevant today as it was 25 years ago. Specifically, the availability of a given advanced technology does not necessarily ensure greater benefit to the child. Without informed application and continual support, the potential benefits of any "cutting-edge," "CD quality," "high-end" assistive hearing technology cannot be realized.

Technology Cornucopia for Children

Our technology has expanded tremendously over the past 25 years or so. As both the number and the quality of technological options have grown, so too have the opportunities for children with hearing loss. Ideally, the assistive hearing technology (or combination of technologies), selected provides the child with the greatest opportunity to use his or her auditory capacity in everyday learning. There is no best technology for all children with hearing loss. The goal in applying technology always transcends the specific means (technology) to achieving the desired outcome. Fortunately, recent developments provide an impressive array of assistive hearing technologies that can be selected to achieve our ultimate goal of intervening with each child. An overview of these developments is provided in the following section.

Developments in Hearing Aids

The choice I had to make in the early 1970s between the Goldentone 5000 and the Leadtone 03 did not challenge my decision-making abilities to any great extent. For the most part, a hearing aid was a hearing aid. Most provided only linear gain (that is, the same amount of amplification regardless of the level of the input signal) and a relatively simple form of output limiting (that is, peak clipping). This is no longer the case. I have provided a list of many of the hearing aid options that are available for application with children today in figure 1. The list seems to grow with each passing day, and, unfortunately, so too does the complexity of the hearing aid selection and fitting process.

- Linear amplification with peak clipping
- Linear amplification with output compression limiting
- Input compression amplification (single band):
  - adjustable compression ratio
  - adjustable compression kneepoint
  - fixed-ratio / variable-ratio compression
- Two-channel hearing aids
  - compression amplification in each band
  - compression amplification in one band / linear amplification in the other
- Three (or more) channel hearing aids
- Directional / multi-microphone technologies
- Digitally programmable hearing aids (1, 2, 3, and more programmable memories)
- Digital signal processing (DSP) hearing aids

Figure 1. Amplification options available in modern hearing aids.

The primary difference among the hearing aid options listed in figure 1 relates to how the hearing aid modifies or processes the incoming sound from the environment. Of course, in all cases, amplification is applied. However, the manner in which sound is processed varies widely across the new generation of "high-tech" hearing aids. A brief discussion of a few basic hearing aid design features may be helpful at this point.

Compression amplification: One of the major developments in hearing aid design in recent years is the extensive use of compression amplification. As noted earlier, a conventional linear hearing aid will apply the same amount of gain (amplification) to all input signals, regardless of level, until the point of amplifier saturation has been reached. I have plotted the input/output function of a linear hearing aid in figure 2. Note that every decibel increase in the input results in an equal increase in output. Thus, the relationship between input to the hearing aid and output is linear or 1 to 1. The decibel difference between the input and output is the amount of gain provided by the amplifier (for example, input: 40 dB + gain: 30 dB = output: 70 dB).

In contrast, a compression hearing aid circuit actively monitors the level of the signal coming into the hearing aid (much as a thermostat monitors room temperature) and automatically adjusts the amount of gain it applies (a hearing aid with a higher IQ!). Note that I have also plotted the input/output function for a compression hearing aid in figure 2. It can be seen that the rate of growth in output is slower for the compression circuit relative to that for the linear gain instrument. The point at which the two curves depart (input: 30 dB SPL) is called the compression threshold or kneepoint. This is the lowest input level at which compression is activated for this particular hearing

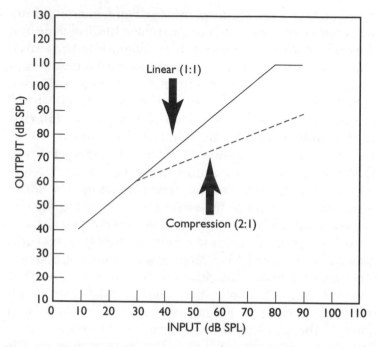

Figure 2. Input / output functions for hearing aids which apply linear amplification and compression amplification.

aid. For the instrument shown, and once the compression circuit has been activated, every 2 decibel increase in the input results in a 1 decibel increase in the output. Consequently we would say that this instrument has a compression ratio of 2 to 1. Both the compression threshold and compression ratio are adjustable in most modern hearing aids.

Generally speaking, input compression hearing aids apply more gain to low level signals (for example, whispered speech) and less gain to high level signals (for example, a shout). The underlying design goal for such hearing aids is to compress or squeeze a wide range of input levels into the relatively narrow hearing range, from threshold to the upper limit of comfort, of a child with hearing loss (Kuk 1996). Consequently, many of the new input compression instruments provide what is often referred to as full- or wide-dynamic range compression (WDRC). In theory, properly fitted WDRC hearing aids should provide children with an audible and comfortable amplified signal across a broader range of input levels. This is because the rate of change in the hearing aid output can be automatically controlled to be one-half, one-third, etc. the rate of change associated with the input to hearing aid. Consequently few, if any, manual volume control adjustments should be required to ensure hearing and hearing comfort (Dillon 1996)—an appealing feature of this new technology for application with children.

With regard to function, modern compression circuits in hearing aids come in variety of shapes and sizes (Dillon 1996). For example, not all compression circuits monitor the level of sound at the input to the hearing aid (input compression). Another common application of compression in hearing aids is in the control of output. This application is often referred to as compression limiting (see figure 1). To protect the ear from level of sound that are potentially uncomfortable or damaging to the ear, all hearing aids employ some form of output control. Compression can be employed at the output stage of the hearing aid amplifier (output compression) to serve this important purpose (Kuk 1996). In addition, some manufacturers employ both forms of compression (input and output) in the same instrument.

Multi-channel hearing aids: To this point in the discussion, only single-channel (sometimes referred to as single-band) hearing aids have been considered. In

such instruments, the form of signal processing selected for the child is applied across all frequencies.
Thus, if a single-channel input compression instrument is selected, the characteristics of the processing
(for example, compression ratio) will be applied across
the full range of frequencies that are amplified by the
hearing aid.

As shown in figure 3, some modern hearing aid
circuits are designed to divide the frequency range
into separate channels (Staab and Lybarger 1994). For
the hearing aid circuit shown in figure 3, the output
from the microphone is separated into two channels—
one allows high-frequency sounds to pass through the
circuit, the other channel is for low-frequency sounds.
The output from these two band-pass filters is then
processed independently and recombined at the output
stage. The frequency that divides the low channel from
the high channel is called the crossover frequency (see
figure 3). The number of channels available in current

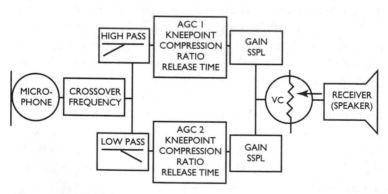

Figure 3. Hearing aid circuit diagram of a two-channel
compression amplifier (from *The Compression Handbook*,
Starkey Laboratories (1997). Reprinted with permission).

hearing aids can range from 1 to 4 (most using between 1 and 3). Multiple channel amplification allows for different signal processing to be used within each of the available bands (Kuk 1996). Thus, as shown in figure 1, compression amplification, in some form, can be employed for one range of frequencies with linear in another. Typically, the range of frequencies which define each channel is under the control of the individual fitting the hearing aid. This technology is used most often in situations where the auditory characteristics of the child vary substantially across frequencies (for example, more hearing loss in the high frequencies than in the low frequencies).

Multi-channel hearing aids have also been proposed as one solution to the problem of hearing speech in a background of noise (Kuk 1996). The operating assumption here is that most of the energy in background noise is concentrated in the lower audible frequencies (below approximately 1000 Hz). A hearing aid with some form of compression amplification in the low-channel will automatically reduce the amount of gain when low-frequency background noise is present. However the amount of amplification the hearing aid provides in the high frequencies (where important acoustic speech cues are present) would remain constant. This amplification strategy assumes that the hearing aid is sufficiently intelligent to know which low frequency sounds we want the child to hear (signal) and which we do not want them to hear (noise). While modern compression hearing aids are smarter than they once were, they are simply not that bright!

Multi-microphone technology: Over the years, a number of different engineering solutions have been employed in hearing aids to improve speech perception in a background of noise. As I noted in the preceding section, multi-channel compression circuits have been proposed as one solution to this problem.

We have known for years that hearing aid microphone design can also be used to improve speech perception in noise under certain listening conditions (Mueller and Johnson 1979; Hawkins and Yacullo 1984). To some extent, what comes out of a hearing aid will depend on what we let in. With this in mind, some hearing aid manufacturers have recently developed special microphones to enhance the perception of speech in a background of noise. In general, regardless of the specific type, directional microphones let in sounds coming from in front of the listener, while suppressing sounds from behind (Staab and Lybarger 1994).

Three microphone designs used in modern hearing instruments are shown in figure 4. An omnidirectional microphone is shown at the top of figure 4. This is the type of microphone used most often. Note that this microphone has only one opening or port. Sound comes into the opening and sets the diaphragm of the microphone into vibration. These vibrations are converted into a small electrical voltage that is subsequently amplified by the hearing aid circuit. When the sensitivity of this type of microphone is tested in an open space (that is, not in place on a child), it can be demonstrated that the omnidirectional microphone is equally sensitive regardless of the direction the sound is coming from.

The microphone shown in the center of figure 4 is a conventional directional microphone. These microphones have been used in some hearing aids since the mid-1970s. Note that this type of microphone has two ports and one diaphragm. An acoustic time delay (shown by shading) is inserted into the port facing to the rear of the hearing aid user (Staab and Lybarger,

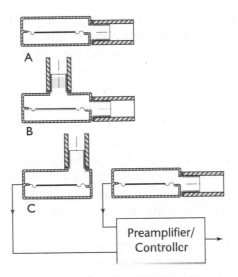

Figure 4. Three microphone types used in modern hearing instruments including: (A) an omnidirectional microphone; (B) a conventional directional microphone: and (C) multi-microphone directional technology (Phonak A/G. Reprinted with permission).

1994). The end result of this microphone design is that sound coming from behind the listener will be reduced relative to sound coming from in front. Consequently, before amplification is applied, sound from the environment has been processed by having the microphone give greater emphasis to acoustic events occurring in front of the child. One known limitation of this type of microphone is that it only reduces low frequency sounds coming from behind the hearing aid user.

The third microphone design shown in figure 4 is an example of the new generation of directional microphone technology (Bachler and Vonlanthen 1995). Note that with this design two separate microphones are used. Consequently, we refer to this as multi-microphone hearing aid technology. The signal processing performed on sound reaching these two microphones is performed by sophisticated hearing aid circuitry. A relative advantage of this new technology is a more uniform reduction of sounds coming from behind the listener across the full range of frequencies. Of course, this particular technology comes with the built-in assumption that what we want a child to hear (signal) comes from somewhere in front of (and not behind) the child. Under some environmental conditions, this is a reasonable assumption to make.

Multi-memory hearing aids: Through the use of multi-memories, the new generation of hearing instruments provides the opportunity to apply different signal processing strategies (for example, omnidirectional vs. multi-microphone technology) under different listening conditions. With these instruments the child or supervising adult can choose among several preset amplification strategies with the simple press of a button on a remote module—not at all unlike choosing which television program you want to watch! This is accomplished by digitally programming each of several different memories in the hearing aid microchip. The number of available memories varies across hearing aids and manufactures. However, depending on the number of memories contained in the microchip, the end result is to have two or more hearing aids in one, each to be used under specific predetermined conditions.

In designing multi-memory hearing aids, the assumption has been that different signal processing or hardware options (for example, FM system input vs. hearing aid microphone input only) are required by children under different communicative circumstances.

Certainly such instruments offer a new level of flexibility in fitting amplification to the hearing requirements of children across a range of environmental conditions. However, I believe that two requirements must be met when considering the possible application of multi-memory technology with any child. First, to take full advantage of the capabilities these systems offer, the audiologist performing the fitting must be knowledgeable about the proper programming of these instruments, and must understand the unique hearing requirements and listening environments of each child. Second, a certain level of user sophistication is required to know which amplification strategy (memory) to use under which specific condition(s). Assuming these requirements are met, such technologies offer opportunities in amplification-related work with children I had not even dreamed of when I began this work in the early 1970s.

Digital signal processing (DSP) hearing aids: For the past 15 years or so, many audiologists have awaited the introduction of true digital hearing aids with growing impatience and sky-high expectations. With few notable exceptions (David Luterman for example), the profession of audiology has had a long history of looking to technology to solve all of the problems associated with deafness in adults and children. Why should digital hearing aids be an exception to this general rule? At the time of this writing, there are at least four high-end digital hearing aids on the market. No doubt, by the time this book has been published there will be several more DSP hearing aids available.

In theory, this new hearing aid technology offers infants and children with hearing loss several potential advantages over conventional analog instruments. The primary advantages are reported to include: (1)

reduction in hearing aid size—the function of various components required in analog amplifiers can now be implemented in a microchip; (2) automatic feedback control; and (3) automatic (and more sophisticated) noise reduction. In addition, DSP hearing aids provide a tremendous amount of fitting flexibility (Schweitzer 1997). Within certain limitations, it is now possible to tell the DSP hearing aid what to do (via programming) and it can be done. Unfortunately, now that we have this highly flexible technology we find that we are not yet entirely certain what we want it to do! Carefully controlled (time consuming / resource intensive) experimental studies will be required before we have the fitting issues all figured out so that we can take full advantage of the DSP hearing aids capabilities.

In the meantime, there is wild enthusiasm in some professional circles for the relative benefits to be derived from this first generation of DSP hearing aids. For example, parents have reported that some hearing aid dispensers have stated that if parents purchase a new DSP hearing aid for their child, the child will need to wear only one hearing aid and that there will be no need for the child to use an FM system in the classroom. I am unaware of any evidence to support such statements. There can be no question that DSP instruments are the future in hearing aid technology and that our ability to fully utilize this technology will improve with time. However, I do expect that in time some of the current enthusiasm will subside as we develop a more realistic understanding of what DSP hearing aids can and cannot do for children with significant hearing loss. It is unlikely, for example, that a child with just a few viable hair cells in the cochlea will obtain any greater benefit from a high-end "CD-quality" DSP hearing aid than he or she will from conventional hearing aids. Fortunately, we now have alternative assistive hearing technologies for the child in this situation, when a hearing aid (DSP or not) is simply not enough.

Developments in FM Systems

Despite several innovative noise reduction strategies that are used in the latest generation of hearing aids, there are environments in which background noise, distance from the signal (for example, parent talking), and/or reverberation in the environment will severely compromise a child's ability to benefit from amplification. One of the most effective signal enhancement technologies available to children for hearing under such difficult environmental conditions is the FM system.

An FM system consists of two basic components: a microphone with an FM radio transmitter for the talker and an FM radio receiver for the child. The signal, a teacher's speech for example, is picked-up by the microphone positioned close to the talker's mouth. The FM transmitter then sends the signal to the child's receiver. The talker's speech is received by the child without any loss in level that would normally result from increased distance and with a minimum of background noise. In this way, FM system technology overcomes the hearing problems introduced by noise, distance, and reverberation. It brings the signal of primary interest directly from its source to the child's ear (Lewis 1994).

Over the years, there have been many improvements to the large, heavy and inflexible body-worn FM systems that were introduced in the 1970s. Examples of these improvements include: (1) development of a range of coupling options to make FM system receivers compatible with a child's personal hearing aids; (2) use of highly directional microphones in the talker's transmitter system; (3) special circuits designed to give greater weighting to signals from the microphone/transmitter relative to sounds received at the environmental microphones worn by the child; and (4) the availability of "low-battery" warning lights.

Of all recent developments in FM system design, perhaps the most important both for ease of use and user acceptance is the substantial reduction in the size of FM system receiver units (Chase and Bess 1996). Four manufacturers now offer systems where the complete FM receiver is located at the child's ear level. For two of these instruments (Phonic Ear Free Ear® and Telex Select® 2-40FM BTE), the receiver unit is housed entirely within the shell of an ear level hearing aid. Two other manufacturers use what is called an FM receiver boot. This is a small FM receiver that snaps onto the bottom of ear level hearing aids and is powered by the hearing aid battery. Examples of this latter option are shown in figures 5 and 6. They include the new Unitron Industries / AVR Communications Unicom® and the Phonak MicroLink® FM systems. This significant reduction in FM system receiver size has been something that both children and parents have been requesting for many years. It is a major development in hearing technology for children and should lead to greater acceptance and use of FM systems by the many infants and children who can benefit from their use (Brackett 1992; Madell 1992; Moeller et al.1996). Finally, it should be noted at this point that FM systems can be used in combination with cochlear implants.

Developments in Frequency Transposition Devices

The mechanism of a piano can be used to understand the potential benefits and limitations of various sen-

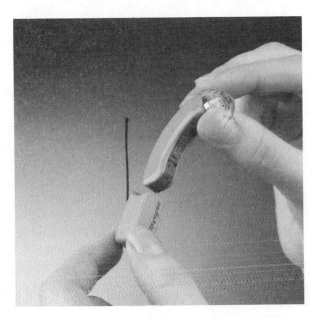

Figure 5. An FM "boot" receiver being connected to an ear level hearing aid (photograph courtesy of Unitron Industries, Ltd.).

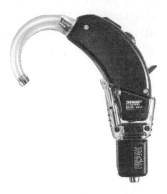

Figure 6. An FM receiver audio shoe (boot) attached to ear level hearing aid (photograph courtesy of Phonak A/G.).

sory aids for children with profound deafness. By pressing the keys on the keyboard, we can produce sounds which range from low to high pitch. The keys can be thought of as sensory receptors—press the key (receptor) and sound is produced by striking the strings of the piano. Now consider the situation in which only one-half of the piano keys are present, the lower half for example. In this case, it is not possible to produce the higher pitch sounds even though the piano strings for those pitches are present. Without the key press (displacement of the sensory receptor), there can be no striking (stimulation) of the strings.

In the case of many children with profound sensory hearing impairment, some or all of the hair cells (auditory keys) are absent, consequently, the nerve fibers leading from the hair cells (auditory strings) are not stimulated. For these children the receptors in the inner ear are sufficiently damaged or underdeveloped which precludes hearing sound at some or all frequencies. If the sensory receptors (auditory keys) are not present, no amount of acoustic amplification can produce audibility within that pitch or frequency range—if you don't have it, you can't use it. Consequently, some children with profound sensory hearing impairment derive little or no measurable benefit from conventional acoustic amplification systems (hearing aids and FM systems). Fortunately there are now viable alternatives to conventional amplification developed specifically for this segment of the population.

To take the piano analogy one step further (and thereby possibly inducing cardiac arrest in an auditory physiologist!), we could think of the pianist's fingers as acoustic energy across a full range of frequencies. The fingers (representing acoustic energy) press the keys (displacement of the hair cells) which in turn leads to striking the strings (stimulation of the auditory nerve fibers leading from the inner ear). In the one-half keyboard example described above, the fingers of the right hand (high frequency acoustic energy) are left with nothing to do. One possible way to circumvent this problem is to use the fingers of both hands (low and high frequency acoustic energy) to play within the range of keys that remain. In this way, sounds of high frequency are shifted downward (transposed) to stimulate the lower frequency receptors that are present. This is the principle that has been applied in the development of transposition hearing aids.

Figure 7 illustrates the principle employed in a transposition hearing aid for a child with no measurable hearing above 2000 Hz. Through the signal processing provided by the transposer device, high frequency sounds (3000 - 6000 Hz) are shifted downward into the lower range of frequencies for which hearing is present. Thus, through this advanced signal processing strategy, the input to the device has been modified to be more compatible with the child's auditory profile.

Several early attempts at developing frequency transposition devices for profoundly deaf children were reported in the late 1960s and early 1970s (Ling and Druz 1967; Ling and Maretic 1971; Erber 1971). I recall listening to one of these devices around 1971. What I heard resembled "acoustic oatmeal." The level of technology available in the early 1970s was simply insufficient to successfully implement this intriguing concept.

Using modern signal processing technology, AVR Sonovation introduced the TranSonic® frequency transposition hearing aid in the early 1990s. At present there are some experimental data on the potential ben-

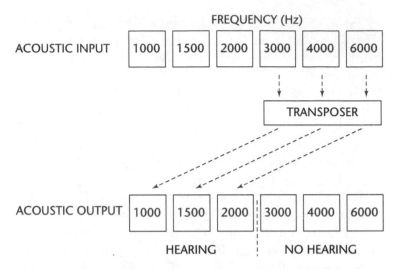

Figure 7.   Simplified illustration of the signal processing strategy applied in a frequency transposition hearing aid.

efits (and some possible limitations) associated with this technology (Chute, Gravel, and Popp 1995; Chute 1997; Parent, Chmiel, and Jerger 1998). An excellent description of the TransSonic® device, including a systematic strategy for fitting children, is provided by Gravel and Chute (1996).

Developments in Cochlear Implants

The first profoundly deaf child received a cochlear implant in 1980 (Osberger 1997). In a chapter I wrote with Mark Ross in the mid-1980s (Seewald and Ross 1988), we reported that 220 children had been implanted as of May 1986. At present (August, 1998) it is estimated that over 8000 children have received cochlear implants worldwide. Cochlear implants are available in over 40 countries at more than 550 cochlear implant centers throughout the world (DeConde Johnson 1998). While

some continue to argue against implanting young profoundly deaf children on ethical grounds (Lane [1993],
for example), there are now sufficient benefit data to
support the application of this technology in children
who are appropriate candidates (Balkany, Hodges, and
Goodman 1996).

Cochlear implant systems consist of both external
and internally worn components. As shown in figure 8,
the primary components that are worn externally in-

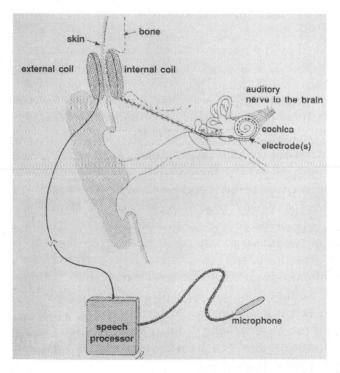

Figure 8.   Illustration of the primary external and internal
components of a cochlear implant (From D. Ling 1989.
*Foundations of Spoken Language for Hearing Impaired
Children*. Reprinted with permission)

clude a directional microphone (worn at ear level), a speech processor and a transmitting coil (external transmitter) containing a small magnet. Components of the system that are worn internally (the implant) include an internal coil with electronic circuitry (internal receiver) for receiving and decoding the signal, and an electrode array. The internal receiver is placed surgically under the skin and embedded within the mastoid bone. The electrode array is positioned in the child's inner ear (cochlea).

Cochlear implant systems work in the following way. Sound from the environment (including speech) is received by the microphone and converted into an electrical signal. The electrical signal is delivered to the speech processor by a thin cable. The processor is programmed to perform its advanced signal processing for each implant user. Once the signal has been processed (filtered, analyzed and coded) it is sent, via a second thin cable, to the external coil and subsequently transmitted via a carrier signal across the skin to the internal receiver. Finally, the internal receiver decodes the signal and delivers it to the electrode array. Electronic wizardry!

The electrode array provides direct stimulation to the nerve fibers in the cochlea, thereby circumventing the problem of missing hair cells (damaged keyboard) within the inner ear. To stretch our piano analogy one step further, one could think of the electrode array as an electronic keyboard programmed to stimulate viable neural receptors (auditory strings) in the cochlea and customized to the characteristics and requirements of each individual.

In the current generation of cochlear implants the electrode array (electronic keyboard) can stimulate up to 20 different locations along the length of the inner ear. The primary advantage of such multichannel implants, relative to the single-channel devices of the late 1970s/early 1980s, is that they can take greater advantage of the natural tonotopic (high to low pitch) design of the inner ear. This enables the user of a multichannel device to extract frequency-specific information that was not previously available through the more primitive single-channel systems. Developments in cochlear implant technology over the past 10–15 years have been nothing short of astounding. Likewise, the benefits many profoundly deaf children derive from implants have increased tremendously and have been well documented through carefully controlled clinical trials (Langman, Quigley, and Souliere 1996; Miyamoto et al. 1996; Geers 1997; Tyler et al.1997; Makhdoum, Snik, and Broek 1997). It needs to be acknowledged, however, that the benefit derived from cochlear implants has been shown to be quite variable (Sehgal et al. 1998). Factors that may underlie this variability include the status of the auditory nerve fibers in the inner ear, the consistency with which the device is used, the quantity and quality of educational management with the implant, and any learning disabilities that may be unrelated to hearing loss.

Recent developments in cochlear implant technology relate to the signal processing strategy applied by the speech processor, as well as to the size of the cochlear implant system components. With regard to signal processing, both the amount and the type of information that is delivered to the electrode array depends on the coding strategy that is applied. In recent years a great deal of research and development effort has been directed toward attempting to improve performance in speech perception by altering the way in which the speech signal is processed by the processor (Skinner et al. 1994). These efforts have been productive and have led to greater benefit from implants in both children and adults (Skinner et al. 1994; Sehgal et al. 1998).

Loeb (1997) has raised an interesting issue concerning signal processing strategies applied currently in cochlear implants. Specifically Loeb points out that new speech-processing strategies tend to be evaluated first in adults, most of whom acquired their deafness later in life. Thus, cochlear implants now employ speech processing strategies designed to "recreate" sensations of sound that adults recognize from prior experiences with acoustic hearing. Loeb argues that because cochlear implants are now used increasingly with prelingually deaf children there is a need to design and evaluate speech processing strategies that are more appropriate for developing nervous systems whose first and only experience with sound comes from electrical stimulation.

Finally, we are now beginning to see a substantial reduction in the size of external components associated with cochlear implant systems. Within the past year, for example, one manufacturer introduced the first ear level speech processor onto the market, thus eliminating the conventional body-worn unit with associated cables—a sign of things to come. The relative advantages of these emerging developments in cochlear implant systems will be apparent to anyone who works with young children.

Developments in Tactile Aids

A purist would not define a tactile aid as an assistive hearing device because these systems circumvent the impaired auditory system completely. However, tactile systems can be defined as a class of sensory aids that are used with profoundly deaf children to enhance speech perception. Consequently, tactile aids are included in this inventory of assistive technologies for children with hearing loss.

It is common to classify tactile aids by the number of tactile transducers that are used and by the mode of stimulation applied. Single channel tactile devices deliver stimulation to the surface of the body via one transducer whereas multichannel systems employ an array of multiple transducers. In addition, the surface of the body can be stimulated mechanically or electrically. Tactile systems that deliver mechanical stimulation are referred to as vibrotactile devices. Tactile systems that deliver an electrical form of stimulation to the skin's surface are called electrotactile devices. Regardless of the specific type of device that is used, all tactile aids transform the acoustic input into a form that can be decoded at some location on the surface of the body. This tactile stimulation can be presented to either the fingers, wrist, forearm, stomach, back or sternum depending on the design of the system (Roser 1989; Cholewiak and Willowitz 1992).

In certain respects, developments in tactile aids have been similar to developments in cochlear implant technology. Much like cochlear implants, the first vibrotactile devices were single channel systems. Modern vibrotactile aids, such as the Tactaid® 7 and the DigiVoc® apply more advanced signal processing by separating the acoustic spectrum of the input signal into multiple channels and delivering the processed output to a vibrator array. The Tactaid® 7 vibrotactile system separates the input spectrum into seven channels whereas the DigiVoc® device provides 16 channels of spectral information. With this new generation of multichannel vibrotactile devices, signal frequency information is coded by the place of stimulation on the skin's surface.

The literature suggests a certain degree of controversy on the benefits to be derived from modern tactile systems, as well as their cost-effectiveness, relative to that offered by cochlear implants (Blamey and Cowen 1992; Osberger et al. 1996; Eilers et al. 1997). There does appear to be general agreement that tactile aids provide benefit to children in speech perception and that the benefit to be derived from these devices is greatest when the tactile information is provided in combination with speech cues received though other sensory modalities such as vision (speech reading) or audition (via hearing aids) (Eilers et al. 1993; Osberger et al. 1996).

In recent years, a number of studies have been conducted in which speech perception and speech production skills have been compared for children using multichannel vibrotactile systems to the performance of children using multichannel cochlear implants (Osberger et al. 1996; Eilers et al. 1997; Ertmer et al. 1997). On the basis of an extensive series of such studies, Osberger et al. (1996) concluded that increasing the number of channels in a cochlear implant results in a significant improvement in speech perception performance. In contrast, for the subjects tested, increasing the number of channels (from 2 to 7) on a vibrotactile device did not result in any additional benefit in speech perception. Further, Osberger et al. report that the average speech perception scores of the multichannel implant users were significantly higher than those of the multichannel vibrotactile users on all speech perception measures that were administered in the "auditory only" or "tactile only" conditions of their experiments. More specifically, Osberger et al. found that the children using multichannel implants were able to correctly identify words presented in an open-set format without the aid of speechreading. However, their findings revealed no evidence of open-set speech recognition for children using tactile aids, even those using a seven-channel device.

Despite the relative degree of benefit that has been demonstrated for multichannel cochlear implant technology, there are profoundly deaf children who, for one reason or another (obstruction in the cochlea due to ossification, congenital malformation of the inner ear, low neuronal stimulability, for example), are not candidates for implantation. For such children, tactile systems may be the most appropriate assistive technology, especially when these devices are used in combination with hearing aids and speechreading.

CURRENT ISSUES IN THE APPLICATION OF HEARING TECHNOLOGIES IN CHILDREN

Early Identification of Hearing Loss does not Ensure Early and Appropriate Intervention with Assistive Hearing Technology

Those who have been around for the past 30 years or so have witnessed on again / off again efforts to identify hearing impairment in early infancy. My own B.Sc. Research Project (Carlin, Seewald, and Wood 1969) was designed to evaluate an innovative newborn infant hearing protocol that had just been reported by Downs and Sterrit in 1967. In that study, we tested the hearing of 100 neonates using a Vicon Apriton portable audiometer. The audiometer had a hand-held loudspeaker capable of producing high-level broad and narrow-band sounds. We presented narrow-band sound of 90 dB SPL to each newborn and watched for a response—eye blink, cessation of sucking, whatever.

Since the days of the "baby blasters" there have been numerous developments in newborn and infant hearing screening procedures including the ABCDs of the newborn nursery (high-risk registers), Crib-o-Grams, auditory brainstem response (ABR) hearing screening systems and, most recently, otoacoustic emission (OAE) test systems. Direct evidence to support universal newborn hearing screening programs was never really there, it just seemed like the right thing to do. The earlier the better premise has been enough to keep the early identification wheels turning for over 30 years. Implicit in the arguments for early identification is the assumption that early identification of hearing impairment leads directly to effective treatment including the timely application of appropriate hearing technology. Some recent data have led some of us to question the validity of this assumption.

Arehart et al. (1998), from the Marion Downs National Center for Infant Hearing, have recently reported the results of a comprehensive survey carried out in 16 states that have implemented universal newborn infant hearing screening programs. This survey investigated the coordination and characteristics of universal newborn hearing screening, audiologic assessment and intervention programs. Of particular concern is the consistent lag time that emerges from the data between the newborn hearing screening and the intervention, including the fitting of amplification. Specifically, 45% of the sites reported that, for infants identified through the universal hearing screening programs, the average initial diagnostic evaluation occurred within the first six months of life. Further, 33% of the sites reported the average age of confirmation of hearing loss was within the first six months of life. However, only 16% reported that the average age at which children were fitted with amplification was within the first six months of life. For over half of the sites (57%), the average age at which intervention was initiated was between 12-18 months of age. Thus, for most, the early identification of hearing impairment did not lead directly to early intervention, a disappointing finding. The substantial delay in treatment with amplification observed in this study has been documented by others (Harrison and Roush 1996).

There are many factors that might delay timely intervention with assistive hearing technologies in infants and young children (Harrison and Roush 1996). Some of these factors are under the direct control of hearing health care professionals, others are not. One factor that we can resolve emerges for the data reported by Arehart et al. (1998). Several items were included in their questionnaire to determine the type of procedures that the pediatric audiologists used in fitting of amplification with infants and young children. It was determined that sound field aided threshold behavioral testing was used by the majority of reporting sites. As Arehart et al. observe, this finding is "interesting" in light of the fact that valid behavioral threshold data are difficult if not impossible to obtain with infants under the age of approximately 6–7 months. They conclude therefore that sites that rely on behavioral audiometric data to fit hearing aids will delay intervention with amplification until the infant (young child, by the time they get it) can perform reliably on behavioral audiometric measures. Alternatives to this conventional behavioral audiometric approach to hearing aid fitting do exist. They have been developed specifically for application with infants and young children (Seewald et al. 1996; Stelmachowicz, Kalberer, and Lewis 1996).

Hedley-Williams, Tharpe, and Bess (1996) reported the findings of a nationwide survey designed to identify and describe current hearing aid fitting practices used by pediatric audiologists in the United States. The survey specifically explored the selection, fitting and verification practices commonly used as well as the types of amplification devices recommended. On the basis of their findings these researchers concluded that few pediatric audiologists in the United States use any systematic approach for selecting and fitting amplification for infants and young children and many do not use current fitting technologies. Many identify hearing impaired children early, fit them late, and fit them (eventually) using procedures which are largely outdated. Those who are interested in learning about contemporary amplification fitting procedures designed specifically for application with infants and young children are referred to the *Position Statement on Amplification for Infants and Children with Hearing Loss* published recently by the Pediatric Working Group of the Conference on Amplification for Children with Auditory Deficits (1996).

The survey data discussed within this section indicate an urgent need to improve the delivery of intervention through assistive hearing technology and other means so that the potential advantages of early identification can be realized. This is something that hearing health care professionals can do something about. As I have noted elsewhere (Seewald 1995): "Regardless of the specific procedures that are applied or the general structure that is associated with the identification program; regardless of the specific device with which a child has been fitted; effective habilitation must be universally accessible to all infants and children and their families. From the consumers' perspective, the identification of a problem without (immediate) access to effective treatment is simply an empty promise."

Which Gizmo for Which Child?: Matching Technology to the Needs of Children

It was not difficult for me in the early 1970s to choose between the Goldentone 5000 and the Leadtone 03. Technology options were relatively limited and consequently so were the opportunities available to children with hearing loss. In contrast, the assistive hearing technology options that are available today are seemingly without limit. This is good. Nonetheless, it must be acknowledged that the massive array of technology that is presently available brings with it new challenges to hearing health care professionals who work routinely with infants and young children. We know that no one technology is best for all children. We do not always know which specific assistive hearing technology is best suited to the characteristics and needs of each child with whom we work. There are several reasons for this.

First, developments in technology outpace research. I am keenly aware of this particular problem because of the contract research I do in collaboration with industry. Over the past several years we have been asked by hearing aid manufacturers to evaluate the benefits derived from a new technology. By the time our research is completed, the manufacturer has already introduced the new "gizmo" onto the market. In most cases, research on the appropriate application of a given technology lags well behind development. Consequently research findings are often not available to support the application of a given technology.

A second problem relates to the capabilities of the target population. Obtaining valid performance measures with infants and young children is extremely difficult, though not impossible (Osberger et al. 1997). I know of very few 6- month-old infants, for example, who will sit happily for an hour of speech perception testing or who will offer a detailed description of their subjective impressions of amplified sound. Assessing the relative benefits of various assistive hearing technologies in infants and young children with hearing loss is not a trivial problem, and it cannot always be assumed that data collected from adults can be used directly in pediatric applications; infants and young children are not just little adults.

Finally, from a research perspective, we are dealing with an enormously complex problem (many variables to be studied and many to be controlled). Consider, for example, all of the amplification options shown in figure 1 that are related to hearing aids alone. All of these various hearing characteristics must be studied as they interact with a potentially large number of child characteristics. As one considers the complexity associated with this problem it is easy to understand why many questions remain unanswered.

One area in which debate is beginning to heat up relates to the increasing trend to place implants in children with more residual hearing and at younger ages. Issues that are beginning to emerge from this debate are both interesting and important to all concerned. Until recently, the criteria for implanting children were relatively straightforward and precisely stated. To be considered as a candidate for a cochlear implant, the old rules stated that a child:

• Must be at least 24 months of age.

• Have a profound sensorineural hearing loss in both ears.

- Receive little or no documented benefit from conventional acoustic amplification.

- Have no medical contraindications for surgical implantation.

- Be enrolled in an educational program that emphasizes the development of auditory skills.

- Have a family that is highly motivated and realistic in their expectations for the implant.

Overtime these rules, largely imposed by the FDA, have been relaxed somewhat. Issues in childhood deafness are rarely if ever "black and white," although they are sometimes presented as such. No doubt, doing away with the old hard and fast rules for implanting children is appropriate and will lead to providing many profoundly deaf children with earlier access to auditory stimulation (Osberger 1997).

There is, however, one related issue that has always been of concern to me - one that will become more important in the days ahead as the age and hearing level criteria for implantation in children are relaxed further. In the past it has been necessary to demonstrate, through formal measures, that children could not benefit from hearing aids before being considered for implantation. The statement went something like this: "Appropriately fitted hearing aids must be used (for some stated period of time) before determining implant candidacy." To my knowledge, few (if any) have ever questioned what is meant by this statement. Certainly it sounds reasonable and appropriately cautious.

The concern I have is that in this field of work, we have yet to agree on an operational definition of "appropriately fitted hearing aids." Let us revisit the survey findings of Hedley-Williams et al. (1996). Recall that these researchers concluded that few pediatric audiologists in the United States use any systematic approach for selecting and fitting amplification for infants and young children, and that many do not use current fitting technologies in the fitting process. A careful examination of the Hedley-Williams data suggests that there is wide practice variation in pediatric hearing aid fitting (many clinicians doing the same thing differently). Consequently, the same child could be seen by five different audiologists and receive five different fittings. Could all five fittings be appropriate for this child? Could all five fittings provide the child with an equivalent degree of benefit? Perhaps, but perhaps not. It is often difficult to determine which of the available assistive hearing technologies is best suited to the needs and characteristics a child even under the best conditions. Consequently, in considering a child for implantation, it is not helpful to perform the all important hearing aid trial with a fitting that may be inappropriate for the child.

Reason for concern regarding the adequacy of pediatric hearing aid fitting practices is supported by some data reported by Chute (1997). In this study, a total of 14 cochlear implant centers in the United States, representing more than 600 children who had been implanted, responded to a questionnaire concerning practices in training, hearing aid fitting and follow-up. Chute reports that, on average, 17% of the children represented in this survey required changes in their hearing aid fittings before implantation would be considered. Further she reported that the percentage of children who required changes in their fittings varied widely across the centers with some reporting fitting modifications in more than 50% of their cases!

Finally, I am particularly encouraged by the recent statement made by a group of individuals (Langman et al. 1996) who work in the implant field. This group recommends that cochlear implant centers must have expertise in applying myriad hearing aid technologies to profoundly deaf children if appropriate recommendations are to be made. Further, they recommend that audiologists who work in implant centers should have the knowledge and experience to select, adjust, and evaluate powerful analog and digitally programmable hearing aids, as well as frequency transposition aids. Of course, these requirements should apply to audiologists in all work settings who work with infants, young children, and their families. The task of improving the quality of pediatric hearing aid fitting is one the entire field needs to embrace. Consequences of the decisions that are made on the basis of the hearing aid fitting will be with the child forever.

In summary, we may not always know the precise answer to the question: which technology for which child? There are some good and some not so good reasons for this. However, if we define the short and long-term goals of our intentions carefully and dedicate ourselves to achieving them, the answers will come in time. To this end, I conclude with Arthur Boothroyd's (1997) clear statement of goals for helping children who have hearing loss through assistive technology.

> The immediate goal of sensory assistance to hearing-impaired children is to provide as much sensory evidence as possible about the sound patterns of speech. This is true regardless of whether the assistance comes in the form of hearing aids, FM systems, cochlear implants, tactile aids or visual speech-training aids. The long-term goal of enhancing sensory capacity is to increase the speed and quality of development - especially the development of spoken language

skills. Success in meeting this long-term goal depends not only on aided sensory capacity, but also on communicative experience, combined with appropriate clinical and educational management. (p. 17)

ACKNOWLEDGMENT

I am grateful to Carol Van Evera, Susan Peters and Susan Scollie for their helpful comments on preliminary drafts of this chapter. Preparation of the chapter was supported by funding to the Hearing Team of the Ontario Rehabilitation Technology Consortium, Ontario Ministry of Health.

CHAPTER 6

Counseling

To work with parents of newly diagnosed deaf children is to begin by working with grief. If counseling is successful, elements of joy later enter the picture. The parents have experienced the profound loss of their expected future; their child and the life they thought they were going to have have figuratively died. For many, the loss is as profound as though someone had actually died.

The most often used description of the grief process can be found in the work of Kubler-Ross (1969) in her observations of the terminally ill. However, the rather straight line progression that she suggests—denial, anger, bargaining, depression, and acceptance—I find to be a bit overused and simplistic for such a complex process. In my experience, there are no set stages in the metaphorical death experienced by parents of deaf children. I find Shapiro (1994), who sees the grief process as crises of identity and attachment, useful for helping parents through their grief. The parents must assume a new identity—that of a parent of a disabled child—and, in the process, they must let go of the notions of themselves as "normal parents." This engenders very strong feelings which need to be examined.

Grief never really ends. In the early stages of diagnosis, there is an active stage of grieving which then becomes chronic sorrow—never to go away completely. Audiologists can facilitate the grief process by the way they conduct diagnostic evaluations. Ideally, the parents are enlisted as collaborators in the diagnostic process and it is they who make the ultimate diagnoses while the audiologist provides emotional support. In this way, as with bereaved families, the parents participation helps mitigate denial. In this chapter, I refer only to hearing parents of deaf children. Shortly after diagnosis of their child's deafness, parents' feelings are often below the level of awareness, buttressed by denial and shock, enabling them to function until they can get to a safe place where emotions often come in a flood. Content-based counseling cannot be successful until parents have opportunities to work through their feelings; when affect is high, cognition shuts off. The operative rule for the counseling model described in this chapter is that feelings are neither good nor bad; they just are, and they need acknowledgment and acceptance—never judgment. Behavior can be judged as to whether or not it is productive; but, we never have to be responsible for how we feel. Armed with this nonjudgmental attitude towards emotions, the clinician can elicit them by empathetic listening.

Feelings

Inadequacy

To be a parent is to be scared. Parenthood is such an awesome responsibility that most parents, when they reflect on what they are doing and what they have done (most prefer not to!), recognize what a daunting task they have undertaken. When they are confronted with an additional problem, such as their child's hearing loss, feelings of inadequacy threaten to overwhelm them in an avalanche of anxiety. These feelings invariably lead to looking outside themselves to be rescued. Consequently, parents will often seek to have the professional assume the responsibility of "fixing" their child. This is always a trap for the professional who wants to help, because, overt help can serve to diminish parents and limit their growth. Overt help always sends a message of incompetency, so feelings of inadequacy are reinforced. It is a professional paradox that often the less one helps, the more the client learns. In a parent group, one father wanted me to be the "quarterback" of his team. When I declined that position, he offered me the coach's job, which I also declined. The only role I would accept was knowledgeable fan, rooting for him and his child on the sidelines. If I made a spectator of him while I called the "plays," he wouldn't learn much or be empowered.

Anger

For many reasons, none of them unreasonable, parents are volcanoes ready to erupt in anger. A major source of anger is the violation of expectations. Parents expect that they will have a normal child, or, at least, that there is a cure for the deafness, and that professionals will solve the problem. Another expectation, also bound to be violated, is that they will be able to resolve this family problem as easily and as well as any of the characters they see on television. When this expectation is dashed—as it is doomed to be—parents experience anger.

Anger also stems from a loss of control which translates into a loss of personal freedom. With deafness, life's options are narrowed. The father who could not accept a desired promotion because his deaf son would not have a good program and the mother who had to stay home to participate fully in her child's education rather than pursue her career, are angry. They have had to give up significant dreams because of the deafness. (At this point, they cannot see what they have gained.) They also feel frustration at their inability to "fix" the deafness.

Anger has survival advantages; much of it, based on fear, mobilizes the body completely for "fight or flight." With anger, we operate at a mid-brain level with the cortex shut off. Anger is useful then, whenever basic survival is threatened. Deafness in a newly diagnosed child threatens the basic structure of the family and can trigger the "fight or flight" response.

Boorstein (1996), a clinical psychologist, has commented: "It is my thesis that with few exceptions, the root of all anger is fear and that psychotherapy is most effective when it focuses on the fears behind the anger rather than on the anger itself." The common fears parents of deaf children have are: (1) Will my child talk? (2) Will my child be independent? (3) Will my child be educated? and (4) Will I be adequate? As professionals working with parents it behooves us to "hang in there" with the angry parent and respond to the fear, rather than to the rage—not easy to do. In most relationships, anger is frequently equated with loss of love, but, actually, there is a great deal of caring in anger: the opposite of love is not hate, but indifference, although this is rarely seen. In most families, because anger is seen as disruptive to family homeostasis, it is not allowed direct expression, so family members often learn to displace it. It is easier and less threatening to a family to be angry at a professional than it is to be angry at a child. (Parents need to realize, at some point, that they are angry at the deafness and not their child; but that, too, takes awhile.) Parents often suppress this anger, something they were taught as children, but, when this happens, they usually become depressed. This depression is not to be confused with the sadness of the loss, that is, a sadness appropriate to the life situation and the pain of the loss that will never go away. Depression based on anger suppression is chronic and pervasive, entering all phases of the parents' lives so that there is no joy in anything.

Professionals can best help angry parents by reflective listening and by responding to the pain of the failed expectations, the loss of control, or the fear. They can help parents most by not feeling threatened by the anger, and responding, instead, to the feelings underlying it. Unfortunately, many of us, like the parents, do not deal well with our own anger or that directed toward us, leading us into defensive postures. When we, as professionals, do this, we fail parents.

Guilt

Nearly every mother of a deaf child who I have worked with experiences guilt over having done something to cause the deafness. Guilt seems to be a "disease" to which women are especially prone. I think it reflects the way women are acculturated, in our society, to powerlessness. Guilt statements, as with worry, are, in reality, statements of power. They are saying "I influenced these events, and, therefore, am responsible"; or "I can influence these events, so I worry about them." This seems to me to be a psychologically expensive way to empower oneself, as it invariably leads to resentment. Guilty people feel controlled by the "other" that is making them guilty. We resent that which limits our degrees of freedom. Unlike anger, which can flare up and ultimately resolve issues through direct conflict, resentment that guilt engenders seems to lurk in the bushes, ever ready to sabotage relationships.

Mothers, in traditional families, usually have the role of safeguarding the health and welfare of the family. So, when someone is "sick," the mother sees this as failure. It is an awesome responsibility to carry a fetus for nine months. In deafness, the cause is often not known (about 50% of the time) so that mothers of deaf children will frequently go over their pregnancy day by day, sometimes hour by hour, to discover what they did to cause the deafness. It is nearly impossible not to have something untoward happen in the nine months of pregnancy that the mother can fixate on as a probable cause of the deafness. As a result, mothers often have a guilty secret. They feel that they did something that caused the deafness; and when they reveal their secret, they give the professional a gift. It means that there is a great deal of trust in the relationship because very often the mother has not told anyone else her secret, including, and sometimes, especially, her husband. Some guilty secrets that parents have shared with me have included: "I smoke and drank during the first trimester." "I took too many saunas." "I ran to catch a bus and that precipitated early labor." Probably, the most devastated, guilt-ridden mother I ever worked with was one who was told by her mother, in growing up, that because she wasn't nice to her older sister, who was deaf, God was going to punish her. And now she had a deaf child! In most families, father guilt is related to his problem-solving role. Fathers see themselves as protectors of the family, and when someone is hurting, they feel they have failed and respond as though they were responsible. This is why most fathers are poor counselors—they are always assuming a fix-it mentality when, very often, all their child or spouse needs is for someone to listen.

The general motif of guilt-ridden parents is that they try to make their child whole again. They are determined to fix it. The appeal of the auditory/verbal methodology to hearing parents is in its promise to restore "normality" to them and their child. This quest for normality based on parental guilt often leads to the super-dedicated parent. We have had several parents in our nursery who, at first blush, look very good. These are parents who often are going to several programs at the same time, seldom missing meetings whether it be in the evenings or on a weekend. They generally have the approval and admiration of the whole staff. Invariably, these families have difficulties later on. So much parental energy has gone into the deafness that there is little left for the marriage or the normally hearing siblings. The marriage becomes a shambles and siblings are at risk. Also, the guilt-ridden, super-dedicated parents find it very hard to let go of their children. So much of their identity has been defined by their child that to let go of it becomes frightening. "If I am not a parent of a deaf child, who am I?"

The other consequence of parental guilt is over-protection. The parent says, in effect, "I let something bad happen to you once; I'm not going to let it happen again." These parents do not let their child develop much autonomy or initiative. They seldom let their child out of sight and they are uncomfortable when they do. The over-protection often extends to the therapy situation by not trusting the competency of professionals. It is hard to maintain a long-term professional relationship with a guilt-driven parent.

In counseling, a professional must deal with the guilt issue in order to establish the intimate, trusting, collaborative relationship between parent and professional necessary for a successful outcome. Non-judgmental listening helps parents talk about their guilt and the reflective responses help parents identify it; here, again, nothing needs to be done other than acknowledge the feelings, and then, as counselors, unhook feelings from unproductive behavior. As one mother told me once, "You know I still have all those unpleasant feelings, but they don't control me anymore." She was a highly successful parent.

Vulnerability

Feelings of vulnerability are very much related to fear and anxiety, but vulnerability has a different dimension. When we get introspective about life—usually at about 4:00 am—we realize our existential aloneness and fragility in what is basically a hostile and meaningless world. This is known as existential "angst," a very uncomfortable feeling. In order to protect ourselves against this, most of us imagine that we are special cases and bad things only happen to other people. Most people prefer to live in a bubble of denial, pretending invulnerability. It is only when something bad happens and denial is futile that people are forced to confront anew their existential angst.

This is what often happens to parents of newly diagnosed deaf children. They undergo an existential crisis in which they realize their vulnerability. Deafness has stripped away their last vestige of emotional protection, and they are frightened. They also undergo a crisis in meaning, as they re-examine their worldview. The traditional view is that God punishes the wicked and rewards the good. If this is true, then why did they have a deaf child? Either God must be bad or they must be bad. For many parents, this is a major crisis requiring, ideally, the help of a caring professional.

On the surface, parents undergoing an existential crisis will look like guilt-ridden over- protective parents. As they recognize how fragile they and their child are, there is a tendency to want to wrap the child in a protective armor. These parents will be asking the "Why me?" or "Why my child?" questions. The existential crisis can have very positive consequences if the therapist allows the parents to work through it without getting caught up in the surface behavior. The truth is that we are all vulnerable, and when we live with this awareness, we don't waste time; we appreciate what we have and can find new meanings and purpose in our lives. I often tell parents deafness is a powerful teacher, and if we listen to it, it can lead us on a path to joy and a better life, albeit along a path of pain and hard work. It seems we must all pay our dues in order to get to a truly joyful place.

Confusion

The initial stages of the learning experience are usually fraught with confusion, as the individual sifts through the information and vocabulary to learn a new skill. This is a natural part of the learning curve, and while sometimes people can get through it quickly, more often than not, especially in the early stages, it seems hopeless and obscure. Such is the task confronting parents as they sort through confusing and conflicting information and opinions, feeling that they must learn quickly or their child will suffer dire consequences.

Audiologists tend to define counseling as information exchange (Flahive and White 1982), and, more often than not, use a medical model of diagnosis which involves taking a case history, testing, and then giving the results of the testing. They bombard the parent with information that cannot be processed because feelings are so high. Martin et al. (1990) have demonstrated, with hard of hearing adults, how little information clients retain at the time of diagnosis.

When I was working as a clinical audiologist, I developed "tapes" for the set lectures I delivered to parents as part of my "counseling." Parents would sit with glazed-over eyes, wanting desperately to be somewhere else, and retaining very little of what I said. As I found on subsequent visits, the lectures, which I thought I had delivered so brilliantly, went in one ear and out the other. At this time, parents are essentially in a state of shock, they have shut down cognitively. Giving information when people are not ready for it only contributes to their confusion and feelings of inadequacy. We do harm with this medical model when it is applied indiscriminately; we would be much more helpful to parents if we asked them what they felt they needed to know and then gave them a chance to talk about their feelings.

With the help of a caring, listening professional, the powerful feelings of parents can be transmuted into positive behavior. Grief becomes a sadness that enables parents to appreciate what they have; anger becomes energy to make changes; guilt becomes a commitment; recognition of vulnerability becomes a means by which parents reorder their priorities; and the resolution of confusion becomes a motivation for learning. Such is the goal of counseling.

Techniques of Counseling

My counseling bias is humanistic, best articulated by Carl Rogers (1951) in what he called "client-centered therapy." I feel this approach can have wide application in our field because it is an approach that places the onus for growth squarely on the client; therefore, it is the most empowering. Other approaches, equally valid, are available, but are beyond the scope of this chapter. Interested readers can refer to my counseling text (Luterman 1995) for more detailed descriptions of those other approaches and techniques. The basic humanistic notion is that within all of us there is a desire to learn and grow called the self-actualizing drive. Wisdom lies within each of us, and only the individual can know what is best for her or himself. The counselor does not presume to know what is best for someone else.

This drive for self-actualization is often thwarted by poor parenting and poor teaching so that the individual is taught not to trust himself and to look outside himself for the "right answer." Another way of putting this is that the locus of control and locus of evaluation is external. These are all the "teacher knows best" and "father knows best" messages children receive. This is not to say that we don't need information that can be provided by external sources. It is the utilization of this information to make meaningful decisions for ourselves that needs to be the responsibility of the individual. People who are on a self-actualizing path tend to have an inner locus of evaluation, while individuals who are not growing tend to externalize evaluation; in short, they dance to others' drumming.

According to Rogers (1951), there are three preconditions for change to take place within a therapeutic environment. First, the counselor must develop an unconditional regard for the client, so that there is maximal psychological safety in the relationship. The client must feel as though he or she could say anything, and it would be accepted in a non-judgmental way.

Secondly, the clinician must practice empathetic or reflective listening. By this Rogers means listening for the "faint knocking." In this, the counselor reflects the feelings of the client conveyed in the message without judgment. If listening is done without empathy, the responses become intrusive and annoying. The third condition is that the counselor must be congruent. By this Rogers means that there should be a strong correspondence between what the counselor is saying and how the counselor is feeling. Another way of saying this is that the counselor needs to be genuine and encourage the development of trust in the relationship. Growth, then, according to the humanistic view, takes place within the relationship—the counselor armed with unconditional regard, empathy, and congruence enters into a therapeutic alliance by creating the conditions that serve to release the client's self-actualizing drive.

For professionals working with the hearing impaired, moving out of the traditional realm of providing content can be frightening, especially when emotional areas are being tapped. However, if one thinks about humanism, it is clear that this is a benign approach. How can we hurt someone by valuing them and listening to them? Webster (1977), a wise speech pathologist, had this to say about the counseling relationship:

> If counseling means the imposition of prescriptions without care for the person for whom they are prescribed, one may, indeed, do damage. The non-accepting, non-compassionate clinician runs the risk of hurting parents; so does the one who focuses concern on the child to the exclusion of concern for the parents. The speech pathologist or audiologist who

leaves to others the interpretation of the information his field has to offer, may do parents great harm. The same can be said for the clinician with limited knowledge who gives faulty information.
On the other hand, it is virtually impossible for one person to damage another by listening to him, by trying to understand what the world looks like to him, by permitting him to express what is in him, and honestly giving him the information he needs. In this view of counseling, the clinician serves as an accepting listener. He delays his judgement and tries to accept parents as they are, and as they will become (p. 337).

Speech and hearing professionals are not counselors for emotionally disturbed people; they are dealing with people who are appropriately emotionally upset, and as such, they can use the knowledge and skills of counseling to help achieve their content mandate. To do this, they must deal with the "upset" first. The essence of the approach to counseling suggested here is listening. Listening is not just not talking; it is putting aside all personal agendas and just being "present." I give a listening assignment to the students in a counseling course I teach, and, initially, they find this extremely hard. In this assignment they are not allowed to talk and have no responsibility to help, other than to be "present," in the dyad where I place them. One person has a problem and talks while the other listens. They, then, reverse roles. When they are not talking in a dialogue, they are usually thinking about what they are going to say next and only listen, at best, with "half an ear." To be truly present for someone else, listening carefully and empathetically, without judgment, is a great gift and the most powerful therapeutic tool we have. The anonymously written poem below says it all.

LISTEN

When I ask you to listen to me
    and you start giving advice
    you have not done what I asked.
When I ask you to listen to me
    and you begin to tell me why I shouldn't feel that way
    you are trampling on my feelings.
When I ask you to listen to me
    and you feel you have to do something to solve my problem,
    you have failed me, strange as that may seem.
Listen! All I asked, was that you listen—
    not talk or do—just hear me.
Advice is cheap: 10 cents will get you both Dear Abby and
    Billy Graham in the same newspaper.
And I can do for myself; I'm not helpless.
Maybe discouraged and faltering, but not helpless.
When you do something for me that I can and need to do
    for myself, you contribute to my fear and weakness.
But, when you accept as a simple fact that I do feel what I feel,
    no matter how irrational, then I can quit trying to convince
    you and can get about the business of understanding what's
    behind this irrational feeling.
And when that's clear, the answers are obvious and I
    don't need advice.
Irrational feelings make sense when we understand what's
    behind them.
Perhaps that's why prayer works, sometimes, for some people
    because God is mute, and He doesn't give advice or
    try to fix things. "They" just listen and let you
    work it out for yourself.
So, please listen and just hear me. And, if you want to
talk, wait a minute for your turn; and, I'll listen to you.

                                   Anonymous

Counseling Caveats

Counseling success is as much dependent on what we do as on what we do not do. Here are some pitfalls.

1. Stereotyping

Stereotyping is a seemingly efficient way of viewing people, if we put them into "little boxes" of characteristics. If we do this long enough, we cease to see who is there and respond only to our expectations of them. I resist all materials that tend to describe characteristics of a particular cultural minority because this leads to cultural stereotyping. In my experience, no two Afro-Americans, Jews, or Hispanics are exactly alike. We are all a marvelous experiment of one! This is especially true of parents. They respond in many different ways to the deafness of their child, and I must put aside my pre-conceptions when I encounter a new parent. For example, some parents who are very cognitively based, need, and can handle, a great deal of information at that initial diagnostic examination, despite what I have written in this chapter. And I need to be sensitive to that possibility. It is always the context of the interpersonal encounter that determines the appropriateness of a professional's behavior.

2. Transference

Transference involves bringing prior learning from the past to the present situation. The Rogers and Hammerstein song, "Some Enchanted Evening," when you see a stranger across a crowded room is supposed to be love. Not to dash romance, but, this is transference. Usually, we transfer characteristics from significant people in our upbringing to the individuals in our present. I give ten additional IQ points to any man who has a moustache like my father's! These transferences can lead us badly astray in our dealings with parents. Whenever I feel strongly about a parent I have just met, either liking or disliking them, that is a red flag for me to step back and see what is going on. I find as I get older, and maybe wiser, I have less transferences. I think that with age, my early life experiences have less influence on my current perceptions; as we get older, we can free ourselves from the past and reinvent ourselves.

3. Projections

Projections are responses to someone else's predicament as though it were our own. All of us are unique, and, although we can empathize with someone else's feelings by listening carefully, we do not know the meaning the events might have for them. They may not respond as we would! I find this especially true as I watch young professional women counseling mothers who are content with the stereotypical "woman's role" of being a mother and passive wife. They often project their values onto her, viewing her as very unhappy, when, actually, she is quite content with her role. It is not for us to judge someone else's marriage, or life for that matter. Projections always lead to being judgmental, which will limit severely the ability to counsel. Whenever we begin thinking that someone else "should" do something, it is invariably a projection. What the "should" means is that we would do that in that situation, but it does not necessarily mean it would be good for the other person.

4. Implicit expectations

Probably nothing impairs relationships more than implicit expectations. This is when we assume that the other person "understands" something we have not said. The parent/professional relationship is fraught with expectations on both sides that need to be made explicit. The biggest source of misunderstanding between parent and professional revolves around responsibility assumption. Parents, very often, believe that it's the professional's responsibility to "fix" their child and that the parental role is to be passive, just providing the funding and transportation, although professionals may feel that their role is to support and "coach" the parent. If they fail to make their expectations explicit and work out a clear contract, the relationship will founder on the shoals of unmet expectations.

5. Overhelping

The more we help people overtly, the less they do, and the fewer opportunities they have to develop their own resources. We give to life what life demands of us, and adversity is our best teacher because it requires us to develop new capacities. With adversity, we can discover within ourselves latent resources that would otherwise lie dormant. Clinicians must find the therapeutic equator of helping each family; we must be gentle coaches. Some families will require little assistance, while others will require much more from us. As good teachers, we want to be on the periphery of what the families are ready to master, armed always with the assumption and attitude that they are competent individuals. Our goal is to empower, and we do this best by not over-helping, but being there in a supportive way. Being able to find the entry point with each family is what distinguishes the superior clinician from the mediocre.

6. Cheerleading

As helping professionals, our instincts are always to take away pain. This is a good and natural instinct, but not necessarily helpful to parents. In deafness, there is nothing that can be done to take away the sense of loss and pain. When we try to do it by cheer-ing people up, telling them it's not so bad, we are invalidating their feelings. We are telling them they have no right to feel this way, and it serves to make them feel guilty, as though something were wrong with them because they do feel this way. By trying to reassure them and tell them that everything will be all right, we lose our credibility. I see this especially with parents of hard-of-hearing children, who are told how "lucky" they are because their child is not deaf, when, in reality, they are not feeling at all lucky. Disability is always in the eye of the beholder—not in the audiogram. I also see "cheering up" with cochlear implants, as though because of these devices, the parents should not mourn because their child can be "cured."

The best thing we can do for parents is to listen to them and give them space and time to mourn their loss. People have marvelous mechanisms for taking psychological care of themselves, and they are very capable of managing their emotional pain; they do it best in the presence of a caring, empathetic listener.

Coping

Grief is a process in which an individual must assume a new identity. Coping is a continuing process as the individual comes to grips with that new identity. Matson and Brooks (1977), in their work with multiple sclerosis patients and their families, proposed a model of coping with a new identity that I have found helpful in my work with parents of deaf children. These stages are not firmly fixed points, but rather a fluid series of sites that are constantly changing, as individuals gain confidence and whenever conditions with the child changes. The four stages are: denial, resistance, affirmation, and integration.

Denial

Probably no single coping strategy has the potential to impair the parent/professional relationship as much as denial. It is a stage of coping, based on feelings of inadequacy, which enable the individual to feel emotionally comfortable in a situation that is perceived as being overwhelming. It is emotional coping, as opposed to problem-based coping. When I am driving my car, for example, and the engine starts making strange noises, I cope by putting on the radio. This makes me feel better, but it does nothing to solve the actual problem. The delay in diagnosing many deaf children is due to parental denial, as they slowly come to realize that there is something wrong with their child. Not only are the parents protecting themselves emotionally by denial, but so are others in their environment, such as friends and grandparents. Even when parents freely acknowledge that their child is hearing impaired, if they do not psychologically "own" the deafness, they are in denial. With parents in denial, hearing aids are seldom worn at home, and if the child is in a total communication program, these parents neither attend signing class nor use sign with their child. The denial mechanism can also cause an adversarial relationship to develop with a clinician who is child focused. The parent is "messing up" the child. The therapist is at a problem-centered coping stage, while the parent is still learning to cope emotionally. You cannot push people out of denial; it only sets up passive resistance. If a professional gives parents an admonishing lecture about how important hearing aids or signing are, the parents will agree but will not substantially alter their behavior. Denial is based on fear, so the clinician must first address parental feelings of inadequacy. When clinicians try to rescue the child from the parents' emotion-centered coping, they do damage because they are reinforcing the parents' feelings of inadequacy. There should never be an adversarial relationship between parent and clinician because both want the same thing. Clinicians must come to see that denial is a necessary coping strategy, and, until we have met parents' psychological needs that denial has imposed on them, we cannot help the child. Try as we might, we can never save children from parental inadequacies.

Resistance

On the surface, resistance looks very much like denial. But, in this stage, the parents psychologically "own the problem." They are still in the "closet", unwilling to reveal to many people that their child is hearing impaired. They believe that they will be a special case, and despite the degree of hearing loss, their child will be "super-deaf" so that nobody will ever be able to tell he or she is hearing impaired. Parents in resistance are shoppers looking for the cure or optimistic prognosis—they are very much attracted to the auditory/verbal approach and its promise of normalization. These parents are very hard, if not impossible, to get into a support group, because they don't identify at all with other parents of deaf children. Parents in denial will go to a support group because they are isolated from their unpleasant feelings, while parents in resistance are very much aware of their pain and do not want to be reminded of it by attending a support group.

Affirmation

In the affirmation stage of coping, the loss is acknowledged both to self and to the world. During this stage, the family is consumed by the disorder. They are very much involved with problem-centered coping and seem to eat, breathe, and sleep deafness. They are easy for professionals to work with and they have fully come out of the disability "closet." In this stage, they are eager to join support groups and national organizations that promote deafness awareness. They possess an intense desire to help others. One mother of a deaf child said, "When you first find out your child is deaf, you feel badly for yourself. After a while you feel badly for your child. Now I feel badly for all deaf children." This movement outside of one's own pain is very healthy and marks the transition into integration.

Integration (Acceptance)

This stage is characterized by getting deafness into a life perspective. It is learning that "beating" deafness is not a matter of reaching normalcy, but rather of living life more fully and authentically with the hearing impairment. The family is changed with a new life style and values; neither is better nor worse than that which they previously had—just different. There is still pain for the loss, and, at times, active grief. These parents, with some training, are ideal mentors for parents of newly diagnosed hearing impaired children and are a largely untapped resource that needs to be used to better advantage.

Families will vary as to the degree and speed with which they can get to integration. Some families seem to move very quickly into the affirmation/integration stages. They are usually families with high self-esteem and good support structures. Some families with a strong religious affiliation also move rapidly to affirmation in that they see the deafness as God's will and they as His instruments. Other families stay stuck in the denial/resistance stages much to the detriment of their child; these families usually have low self-esteem and poor support structures. I also see this as a failure on the part of professionals to counsel adequately and help these families move through the coping process. The key, again, as I have said repeatedly throughout this text, is the self-esteem of the family—especially the mother, because she usually assumes responsibility for the education of the child in most families. If you have an empowered mother with high self-esteem, you will generally have a successful child; all our clinical endeavors need to be devoted to increasing the self confidence of the mother.

Some specific counseling techniques need to be mastered. I am always leery about teaching techniques because a clinician can become so self-conscious that he or she fails to listen, and thereby loses authenticity. If a clinician is not listening to a parent or is not genuine, no number of techniques will help. With that in mind, here are some things to think about when interacting with parents. How we respond to a parent's comment or question will determine the quality of the interaction. We can respond with content, counter question, affect, reframing, sharing self, or affirmation. Each response can steer the relationship in a different direction. There is no right or wrong response. How and when the response is given is just as important as what is said. Timing is everything. The context of the interaction will determine the appropriateness of the response.

Content level responses generally keep the relationship at an expected and rather predictable level and are the ones most commonly used by professionals. Although we have a mandate to provide information to parents, too much content, when given too

early, tends to confuse parents and fuel their feelings
of inadequacy. It is generally best to wait for content
question from the parent, but it is not always easy to
identify a parent's question as content seeking.

More often than not when people are asking questions, they are not seeking content. They want confirmation of a decision they have already made and are
hoping you will confirm. For example, an Hispanic
mother of a newly diagnosed deaf child asked me if
she came into our program would she have to speak
English to her child? I could have responded with content, stating how much better it would be if she did
speak English and not confuse him with several different language systems. Instead, I asked her what she
planned to do, and she told me that her husband and
she decided that if we made them speak English at
home, she wasn't going to come into the program. I
told her that she could do at home what she thought
best—in the nursery we would speak English to him.
She agreed. A few months later, she announced to the
parents' group that she and her husband had decided
to speak English at home to her son. At the time of diagnosis, it was too soon for her to have to give him up
both as a hearing child and as a culturally different
child. Hearing parents of deaf children have the same
problem when introduced too early to members of the
culturally deaf community. Later, when they are in the
affirmative stages of coping, they will be better prepared to listen to the message. When parents are emotionally ready, they will find the best solutions on their
own, if we give them time within a non-judgmental,
supportive environment.

When parents are seemingly asking for advice or
an opinion, more often than not they are seeking confirmation. Questions such as, "Is a particular program

or method a good one?" are best responded to with a counterquestion. "Have you visited the school?" Or "What is your thinking about that method?" When we blunder ahead proudly displaying how smart and knowledgeable we are, we invariably wind up putting our feet in our mouths. When we are so wedded to a particular method or program that we become salesmen, we can set up an adversarial or dependent relationship. Neither one is helpful. The hardest thing for most professionals to learn is that they do not have to answer every question, and in most cases it is better not to.

Hearing the "faint knocking" hinted at by the parent's statement comes closest to describing what Carl Rogers called reflective listening. This kind of listening can open the relationship dramatically because it alleviates the loneliness that most parents feel because now somebody hears and seems to understand. Thus, the parent who says to me "If this was your child, what would you do?" might get the response from me "That's an awesome responsibility you are feeling now isn't it? Why don't we talk about that?" The conversation then can go in the more fruitful direction of discussing the parents' fears and developing criteria for selecting a program. These kinds of responses are most frightening to professionals because they do move the relationship into the emotional realm, a place where little training has taken place. Sabbeth and Leventhal (1988) wrote about the "trial balloons" that patients and families send up when they interact with their doctor. They believe that it is a physician's responsibility to respond to patients' feelings. I have found that even when I miss the mark, my response can still be helpful in assisting parents to clarify how they are feeling. Affect level responses require time, and are not to be attempted in a time-limited context; these responses open up areas that will need considerable follow-up and exploration.

Reframing is also a powerful response that requires careful timing. All events that happen to us are mediated by our perceptions of them. In short, it is we who give meaning to events in our lives. We, therefore, have choices (although it often does not feel like it) of how we want to see something. This is the old conundrum of the half full or half empty glass. The answer lies in how we choose to see it. A reframing response helps parents change their perception. It causes a psychological "jolt." To parents of a newly diagnosed deaf child, I might comment "Well, this child has saved you from a dull life." Or to the parent who is saying, "Why me?" I might respond, "Why not you? What is so special about you that you should not have a deaf child?" To a mother complaining that her husband wouldn't do lessons with their child, but only played with her, I commented, "Thank God someone in the family was treating her as a child." To the guilt-ridden mother who is upset because she did not diagnose the deafness until her child was one year old; "What a nice gift you had of enjoying your child for a year." All of these responses lead to some very fruitful discussions. As always, it is the timing and the context that determine how successful a response is.

Sharing oneself is a response that humanizes a professional. It indicates to the parent that we are two persons collaborating to help the child. Sometimes, not too early in the relationship, it may be fruitful and empowering to ask parents for help regarding their child. One parent once said, "I love to go to school and see the teacher have difficulty with my child; it validates my own experience." When we are seemingly so competent in all we do, this very often diminishes the parent. We also can share how we feel about the family, including getting angry at them if they violate an explicit expectation, or, conversely, tell them how much they mean to us. What I am seeking in the sharing self response is a genuineness in the relationship as opposed to the artificiality found in training programs that stress being "professional." One can be competent and human at the same time. The affirmative response is probably the most powerful of all. It is the "uh-huh." It is saying to parents I am here; tell me more. It is the listening response; and in many of my interactions with parents, it is the only response I need give, as they work out their problems for themselves. How nice it is to be listened to, but how unsettling it can be because it so rarely happens.

Another technique that I find especially useful is in the realm of language changes. The words we use are reflections of our attitudes about ourselves. These words can be empowering and reflect an inner locus of control, or they can be passive, reflecting an external locus. Words, such as "should," "ought," "lucky," and "have to" are red flags for me, indicating a sense of powerlessness. I am always modeling empowered language and, if need be, gently suggesting that parents might change the sentence, "I *ought* to talk to the audiologist" to "*choose* to." "Lucky" people seldom take credit for the good they do; usually, they take all credit for the bad, and, instead of saying, "I am lucky to have found this program," they can be gently persuaded to say "How smart I was to have located this program." Language changing must be done gently and carefully, and never when feelings are running high, because it forces the person back into a cognitive stance, and often can be seen as annoying rather than helpful. I delight when parents (and students, too) begin to use empowered language spontaneously. It reflects the success of the counseling.

Time management is always an issue related to the setting of boundaries. I am always very careful about letting people know how much time is available for our meeting. I might say to a parent, "We have 15 minutes; how do you want to use this time?" I have found, supported by research (Munro and Bach 1975) that time-limited counseling is more effective than when no limits are set. People work harder and use their time better when they know that there is a limited amount of it. (This is true of our lives; if we live with death awareness, we live our lives better.) When counseling both parents (or partners), as is often done at the initial diagnostic evaluation, it should bo rc membered that most marital relationships have a complementary or reciprocal arrangement—if one member of the marital pair is highly emotional, the other will almost always be very cognitive. Some of this is by design, as we tend to seek in our marital relationships persons who complement us, whose traits we admire because they are lacking in us. (In a good long-lasting relationship, we increase our congruence by learning from our mate.) This situation also dictates our behavior if one parent is emotionally distraught, the other will have to "hold it together." Someone has to be concerned about the insurance and be able to drive home, and it one spouse is an emotional "basket case" with limited cognitive ability, then the other spouse will assume a cognitive stance.

Over time, things usually even out in the relationship. The guilt-ridden mother, for example, who was sure God punished her because she was not nice to her deaf sister, was, for a long time, an emotional basket case. She cried copiously in every support meeting for the first few months. She also complained about her husband who was always a "cheerleader"—telling her that everything would be all right. Toward the end of the semester, as she began to feel better, she told the support group the following anecdote:

> Last night I was preparing dinner, and I had the radio on quite loudly. My husband came home and told me to lower the volume as it would wake the baby. I told him "You can't wake the baby; she's deaf." He got the strangest expression on his face and then he began to cry. He wept all night. That was the first time I saw him cry.

I commented that now, because she was feeling better, it looked as if he had some space to mourn. In an unhealthy relationship, parents get locked into their roles and, very often, the counselor has to release the father from his "protective role" to allow him to mourn. This usually happens in due course, as in this case, when the mother becomes empowered. When it does not happen, more active intervention is needed.

It is always clinically profitable to pay attention to the marriage, because it is the linchpin of the family. I have found, over the years, that the most successful children in our program have been the products of happy marriages. Rearing a deaf child successfully requires an enormous amount of energy, and parents will have to get sustenance from someplace—usually in the marriage.

Single parents can do the job well, too, but they will need to develop a strong social support network to succeed. Over the years, I have seen successful single parents get the support they need from their own parents and from their siblings. When family cannot help, the program must provide more support than it does with intact families. The therapeutic context always determines the most appropriate professional response and each family must be treated as a marvelous experiment of one.

The humanistic philosophy suggested in this chapter does not relegate the counselor to being a marshmallow. We can be accepting and non-judgmental, and at the same time, have a firm sense of boundary. There are core values that I do not compromise, such as those regarding assumption of responsibility and the parent or caregiver's active involvement in the therapy process. Other issues are negotiable, such as the amount of time a family has to come to the program or which caregivers attend. What humanism does demand is that the professional continue his or her own personal growth; all good technique stems from personality. It is embedded within the congruence of the counselor. It is not a mantle that a professional puts on when a client is present and then discards the rest of the time. We have as much responsibility to our clients to continue growing as people as we do in learning about the latest techniques in therapy. Unfortunately, very little training in counseling takes place in our universities. A recent survey by Crandell (1997) estimates that only about 18% of graduating audiologists take a course in counseling. With the rapid changes taking place in the education of the deaf, with a new emphasis on early detection and early intervention, both audiologists and speech pathologists are going to need enhanced counseling skills. Unfortunately, it does not seem to be happening. A recent survey by Culpepper et al. (1994), which was a follow-up study on an earlier survey of training programs, found that there was little growth in the number of programs offering a counseling course. Too many of our graduates are leaving programs without being exposed to good counseling techniques—and clients suffer as a consequence. It behooves us, as professionals, to seek out those personal growth and academic experiences that will enhance our counseling skills. We owe our clients no less.

References

Abdala de Uzcategui, C. and Yoshinaga-Itano, C. 1997. Parents'
reactions to newborn hearing screening. *Audiology Today*
9(1):24–25.

Arehart, K. H., Yoshinaga-Itano, C., Thompson, V., Gabbard, S.
A., and Brown, A. S. 1998 (in press). State of the states: The
status of universal newborn hearing identification and intervention systems in 16 states. *American Journal of
Audiology.*

Aldridge, L. 1981. *Family Learning Implementation Guide.* Washington, D. C.: Gallaudet University Press.

Dabidge, II. S. 1965. *Education of the Deaf.* A report to the
Secretary of Health, Education, and Welfare by his Advisory
Committee on The Education of the Deaf. Washington, DC:
U. S. Government Printing Office, 0-765-119.

Bachler, H., and Vonlanthen, A. 1995. Audio-Zoom processing for
improved communication in noise. Phonak Focus 18:3–18.

Balkany, T., Hodges, A., and Goodman, K. W. 1996. Ethics of
cochlear implantation in young children. *Otolaryngology -
Head and Neck Surgery* 114(6):748–55.

Barnum, M. 1984. In support of bilingual/bicultural education for
deaf children. *American Annals of the Deaf* 129:404–408.

Bender, R. 1981. *The Conquest of Deafness.* Danville, IL: Inter-
state Publishers.

Bess, F., and Paradise, J. 1994. Universal screening for hearing
impairment: Not so simple, not risk-free, not necessarily
beneficial and not presently justified. *Pediatrics* 93(2):
330–34.

Blamey, P. J., and Cowen, R. S. 1992. The potential benefit and
cost-effectiveness of tactile devices in comparison with
cochlear implants. In *Tactile Aids for the Hearing Impaired,*
ed. I. R. Summers. London: Whurr Publishers.

Bloom, L. 1974. Talking, understanding and thinking. In *Language Perspectives-Acquisition, Retardation, and Intervention*, eds. R. L. Schiefelbusch and L. L. Lloyd. Baltimore, MD: University Park Press.

Bodner-Johnson, B. 1986. The Family in Perspective. In *Deafness in Perspective*, ed. D. Luterman. San Diego CA: College-Hill Press.

Bodner-Johnson, B., and Sass-Leher, M. 1996. Concepts and premises in family school relationships. Pre-College National Mission Programs. Washington, DC: Gallaudet University

Boorstein, S. 1996. *Transpersonal Psychotherapy*. Albany, NY: State University of New York Press.

Boothroyd, A. 1997. Auditory capacity of hearing-impaired children using hearing aids and cochlear implants: Issues of efficacy and assessment. *Scandinavian Audiology* 26 (supplement 46):17–25.

Brackett, D. 1992. Effects of early FM use on speech perception. In *FM Auditory Training Systems: Characteristics, Selection and Use*, ed. M. Ross. Timonium MD: York Press.

Brown, A. S., and Yoshinaga-Itano, C. 1994. F.A.M.I.L.Y. Assessment, a multi-evaluation tool. In *Infants and Toddlers with Hearing Loss*, ed. J. Roush and N. D. Matkin. Baltimore: York Press.

Bruce, R. 1973. *Bell: Alexander Graham Bell and the Conquest of Solitude*. Boston: Little, Brown.

Bruner J. 1974. The ontogenis of speech acts. *Journal of Child Language* 2:1–19.

Bruner, J. 1983. *Child's Talk: Learning to Use Language*. New York and Oxford: Oxford University Press.

Carlin, T. W., Seewald, R. C., and Wood H. 1969. Neurological implications of responses of neonates to auditory stimuli. *The Guthrie Clinic Bulletin* 38(4): 189–93.

Carney, A., and Moeller, M. P. 1998. Treatment efficacy: Hearing loss in children. *Journal of Speech and Hearing Research* 41:561–84.

Chase, P. A., and Bess F. H. 1996. Behind-the-ear FM systems: New technology for children. In *Amplification for Children with Auditory Deficits*, eds F. H. Bess, J. S. Gravel, and A. M. Tharpe. Nashville TN:Bill Wilkerson Center Press.

Cholewiak, R. W., and Wollowitz, M. 1992. The design of vibrotactile transducers. In *Tactile Aids for the Hearing Impaired*, ed. I. R. Summers. London:Whurr Publishers.

Chute, P. M. 1997. Timing and trails (?) of hearing aids and assistive devices. *Otolaryngology-Head and Neck Surgery* 117(3):208–13.

Chute, P. M., Gravel, J. S., and Popp, A. 1995. Speech perception abilities of adults using a multichannel cochlear implant and frequency transposition hearing aid. In *International Cochlear Implant, Speech and Hearing Symposium. Melbourne 1994: Annals of Otology, Rhinology and Laryngology*, eds. G. Clark and R. Cowen. Supplement 166, 104:260–63.

Cole, E. 1994. Encouraging intelligible spoken language development in infants and toddlers with hearing loss. *Infant Toddler Intervention, The Transdisciplinary Journal* 4(4):263–84

Cole, E. B. 1992. *Listening and Talking: A Guide to Promoting Spoken Language in Hearing Impaired Children*. Washington, DC: Alexander Graham Bell Association for the Deaf, Inc.

Cole, E. B. 1992. Promoting emerging speech in birth to 3 year-old hearing-impaired children. *Volta Review* 94:63–77.

Cornett, O. 1967. Cued speech. *American Annals of the Deaf* 112:3–13.

Crandell, C. 1997. An update on counseling instruction within audiology programs. *Journal of the Academy of Rehabilitative Audiology* 30:1–10.

Culpepper, B., Mendel, L., and McCarthy, P. 1994. Counseling experience and training offered by ESB-accredited programs. *ASHA* 36:55–64.

DeCasper, A. J. and Feifer, W. P. 1980. Of human bonding: Newborns prefer their mothers' voices. *Science* 208:1174–6.

DeConde Johnson, C. 1998. Pediatric cochlear implant fact sheet. *Educational Audiology Review* 15(1):7–8.

DeVilliers, P. A., and J. G. 1979. *Early Language*. Cambridge, MA: Harvard University Press.

Dillon, H. 1996. Compression? Yes, but for low or high frequencies, for low or high intensities, and with what response times? *Ear and Hearing* 17(4):287–307.

Downs, M. P. 1995. Universal newborn hearing screening—the Colorado story. *International Journal of Pediatric Otorhinolaryngology* 32:257–59.

Downs, M. P., and Sterrit, G. M. 1967. A guide to newborn and infant hearing screening programs. *Archives of Otolaryngology* 85:15–22.

Dunst, C. J., Wortman Lowe, L., and Bartholomew, P. 1990. Contingent social responsiveness, family ecology and infant communicative competence. *National Student Speech Language Hearing Association Journal* 17:39–49.

Eilers, R. E., Vergara, K., Oller, D. K., and Balkany, T. J. 1993. Evaluating hearing-impaired children's usage of tactile vocoders. In *Proceedings of the Second International*

Conference on Tactile Aids, Hearing Aids and Cochlear Implants. Stockholm: Akademitryck AB.

Eilers, R. E., Cobo-Lewis, A. B., Vergara, K. C., and Oller D. K. 1997. Longitudinal speech perception performance of young children with cochlear implants and tactile aids plus hearing aids. *Scandinavian Audiology* 47(suppl):50–54.

Eimas, P. D. 1974. Linguistic processing of speech by young infants. In *Language Perspective: Acquisition, Retardation and Intervention*, eds. R. L. Schiefelbusch and L. L. Lloyd. Baltimore: University Park Press.

Elssman, S., Matkin, N., and Sabo, M. 1987. Early identification of congenital sensorineural hearing impairment. *Hearing Journal* 40:13–17.

Engen, T., Engen, E., Clarkson, R. L., and Blackwell, P. M. 1983. Discrimination of intonation by hearing impaired children. *Journal of Applied Psycholinguistics* 4:149–60.

Erber, N. P. 1971. Evaluation of special hearing aids for deaf children. *Journal of Speech and Hearing Disorders* 36:527–37.

Erber, N. P. 1982. *Auditory Training*. Washington, DC: Alexander Graham Bell Association for the Deaf, Inc.

Erikson, E. 1950. *Childhood and Society* (2nd ed.). New York: Norton.

Ertmer, D. J., Kirk, K. I., Sehgal, S. T., Riley, A. I., and Osberger, M. J. 1997. A comparison of vowel production by children with multichannel cochlear implants or tactile aids: Perceptual evidence. *Ear and Hearing* 18(4):307–15.

Farrugia, D., and Austin, G. 1980. A study of social-emotional adjustment patterns of hearing impaired students in different educational settings. *American Annals of the Deaf* 125:535–41.

Feher-Prout, T. 1996. Stress and coping in families with deaf children. *Journal of Deaf Studies and Deaf Education* 1(3):155–66.

Fernald, A. and Kuhl, P. 1987. Acoustic determinants of infant preference of motherese speech. *Infant Behavior and Development* 10:279–93.

Flahive, M., and White, S. 1982. Audiologists and counseling. *Journal of the Academy of Rehabilitative Audiology* 10:275–87.

Flexer, C., Gray, D., Millin, J., and Leavitt, R. 1993. Mainstreamed college students with hearing loss: Comparison of receptive vocabulary to peers with normal hearing. *Volta Review* 95:125–33.

Gallaudet, E. M. 1997. Is the sign language used to excess in the teaching of deaf mutes? *American Annals of the Deaf* 142(3):21–23.

Gallaudet, E. M. 1997. Must the sign language go? *American Annals of the Deaf* 142(3):31–34.

Garvey, C. 1977. *Play.* Cambridge, MA: Harvard University Press.
Gatty, J. 1994. The VIP program, Clarke School. In *Infants and Toddlers with Hearing Loss*, eds. J. Roush and N. D. Matkin. Timonium MD: York Press.
Goldstein, M. 1939. *The Acoustic Method.* St. Louis: The Laryngoscope Press.
Gravel, J. S., and Chute, P. M. 1996. Transposition hearing aids for children. In *Amplification for Children with Auditory Deficits*, eds. F. H. Bess, J. S. Gravel, and A. M. Tharpe. Nashville TN: Bill Wilkerson Center Press.
Geers, A. E. 1996. Comparing implants with hearing aids in profoundly deaf children. *Otolaryngology - Head and Neck Surgery* 117(3):150–54.
Greenstein, J. 1975. *Methods of Fostering Language Development in Deaf Infants: Final Report* (BBB00581). Washington, DC: Bureau of Education for the Handicapped (DHEW/OE).
Harris, M., and Mahoney, H. 1997. Learning to look in the right place: A comparison of attentional behavior in deaf children with deaf and hearing mothers. *Journal of Deaf Studies and Deaf Education* 2(2):95–103.
Halpern, K. 1989. Hearing and deaf parents' reactions to deaf ness. Unpublished master's thesis, Emerson College, Boston MA.
Harrison, M., and Roush, J. 1996. Age of suspicion, identification and intervention for infants and young children with hearing loss. A national survey. *Ear and Hearing* 17(1):55–62.
Hawkins, D. and Yacullo, W. 1984. Signal-to-noise ratio advantage for binaural hearing aids and directional microphones under different levels of reverberation. *Journal of Speech and Hearing Disorders* 49(3):278–86.
Hedley-Williams, A., Tharpe, A. M., and Bess, F. H. 1996. Fitting hearing aids in the pediatric population: A survey of practice procedures. In *Amplification for Children with Auditory Deficits*, eds. F. H. Bess, J. S. Gravel, and A. M. Tharpe. Nashville TN: Bill Wilkerson Center Press.
Hermann, B. 1994. Perspectives and implications of early identification of hearing loss. *Current Opinion in Otolaryngology and Head and Neck Surgery* 2:449–54.
Hermann, B., Thorton, A., and Joseph, J. M. 1995. Automated infant hearing screening using the ABR: Development and validation. *American Journal of Audiology* 4:6–14.
Hnath-Chisolm, T. 1997. Context effects in auditory training with children. *Scandanavian Audiology*, Vol 26, suppl 47:64–69.
Johnson, R. C., and Cohen, D. 1994. Implications and complication for deaf students of the full inclusion movement.

Gallaudet Research Institute (Occasional Paper 94-2). Washington DC: Gallaudet University.

Johnson, R. E., Liddell, S., and Erting, C. 1989. Unlocking the curriculum: Principles for achieving access in deaf education. Gallaudet Research Institute (Working paper No. 89-3). Washington, DC: Gallaudet University.

Jordan, I. K., Gustason, J., and Rosen, R. 1979. An update on communication trends in programs for the deaf. *American Annals of the Deaf* 124:350–57.

Jusczyk, P. W. 1995. Language acquisition: Speech sounds and phonological development. In *Handbook of Perception and Cognition, Vol 11: Speech, Language, and Communication*, eds. J. L. Miller and P. D. Eimas. Orlando: Academic Press.

Jusczyk, P. W., Cutler, A., and Rednaz, L. 1993. Infants' sensitivity to predominant stress patterns in English. *Child Development* 64:675–87.

Jusczyk, P. W., Luce, P., and Charles-Luce, J. 1994. Infants' sensitivity to phonotactic patterns in native language. *Journal of Memory and Language* 33:630–45.

Koester, L. S., and Meadow-Orlans, K. P. 1990. Parenting a deaf child: Stress, strength, and support. In *Educational and Developmental Aspects of Deafness*, eds. D. F. Moores and K. P. Meadow-Orlans. Washington, DC: Gallaudet University Press.

Kubler-Ross, E. 1969. *On Death and Dying*. New York: Macmillan.

Kublin, K. S., Wetherby, A..M., Crais, E. R., and Prizant, B. M.. 1998. Prelinguistic dynamic assessment: A transactional perspective. In *Transitions in Prelinguistic Communication*, eds. A. M.. Wetherby, S. F. Warren and J. Reichle, Baltimore, MD: Paul H. Brookes Publishing Co.

Kuk, F. K. 1996. Theoretical and practical considerations in compression hearing aids. *Trends in Amplification* 1(1):5–39.

Lane, H. 1993. *The Mask of Benevolence*. New York: Vintage Books.

Lane, H., Hoffmeister, R., and Bahan, B. 1996. *A Journey into the Deaf World*. San Diego: Dawn Sign Press.

Langman, A. W., Quigley, S. M., and Souliere, C. R. 1996. Cochlear implants in children. *Pediatric Otolaryngology* 43(6): 1217–31.

Lederberg, A. R., and Everhart, V. S. 1998. Communication between deaf children and their hearing mothers: The role of language, gesture, and vocalizations. *Journal of Speech Language Hearing Research* 41:887–99.

Lewis, D. E. 1994. Assistive devices for classroom listening. *American Journal of Audiology* 3:58–69.

Loeb, G. E. 1997. Speech processing strategies designed for children. *Otolaryngology - Head and Neck Surgery* 117(3):170–73.

Ling, D. 1976. *Speech and the Hearing Impaired Child: Theory and Practice*. Washington, DC: Alexander Graham Bell Association for the Deaf.

Ling, D. 1989. *Foundations of Spoken Language for Hearing-Impaired Children*. Washington DC: A. G. Bell.

Ling, D. 1993. Auditory-verbal options for children with hearing impairment: Helping to pioneer an applied science. *The Volta Review* 95:197–204.

Ling D., and Druz, W. S. 1967. Transposition of high frequency sounds by partial vocoding of the speech spectrum: Its use by deaf children. *Journal of Auditory Research* 7:133–44.

Ling, D., and Maretic, H. 1971. Frequency transposition in the teaching of speech to deaf children. *Journal of Speech and Hearing Research* 14:37–46.

Luterman, D. 1987. *Deafness in the Family*. Boston: Little Brown.

Luterman, D. 1990. Audiological counseling and the diagnostic process. *ASHA* 32:35–37.

Luterman, D. 1994. The Thayer Lindsley Family Centered Nursery. In *Infants and Toddlers with Hearing Loss*, eds. J. Roush and N. D. Matkin. Timonium MD: York Press.

Luterman, D. 1995. Counseling for parents of children with auditory disorders. In *Auditory Disorders in School Children*, eds. R. Roeser and M. Downs. New York: Theme Publishers.

Luterman, D. 1995. *Counseling Persons with Communication Disorders and Their Families*. Austin TX. PRO-ED.

Luterman, D., and Kurtzer-White, E. 1998. Parents' views of management: Part II. *American Journal of Audiology* (accepted for publication).

McLean, L. S. 1990. Communication development in the first two years of life: A transactional process. *Zero to Three* 11:13–19.

Madell, J. 1992. FM systems for children birth to age five. In *FM Auditory Training Systems: Characteristics, Selection and Use*, ed M. Ross. Timonium MD: York Press.

Makhdoum, M. J., Snik, A. F., and van den Broek, P. 1997. Cochlear implantation: A review of the literature and the Njmegen results. The *Journal of Laryngology and Otology* 111:1008–17.

Mankowitz, J., and Larson, M. 1990. A longitudinal study of children in preschool special education programs. *Research in Education* 3:120–7

Martin, E., Kruegar, S., and Bernstein, M. 1990. Diagnostic information transfer to hearing impaired adults. Texas *Journal of Audiology and Speech Pathology* 16(2):29–32.

Mason, J., And Hermann, K. 1998. Universal infant screening by automated auditory brainstem response measurement. *Pediatrics* 101(2):221–28.

Matson, D., and Brooks, L. 1977. Adjusting to multiple sclerosis: An explorative study. *Social Science and Medicine* 11:245–50.

Mauk, G. W., and White, K. R. 1995. Giving children a sound beginning: The promise of universal newborn hearing screening. *Volta Review* 97:5–32.

Mauk, G. W., White, K. R., Mortensen, B. R., and Behrens, T. R. 1991. The effectiveness of screening programs based on high-risk characteristics in early identification of hearing impairment. *Ear and Hearing* 12:312–19.

Maxon, A. B., White, K., Behrens, T., and Vohr, B. 1995. Referral rates and cost efficiency in a universal newborn hearing screening program using transient evoked otoacoustic emissions. *Journal of American Academy of Audiology.* 6:271–77.

Maxon, A. B., White, K., Culpepper, B., and Vohr, B. 1997. Maintaining acceptably low referral rates in TEOAE-based newborn hearing screening programs. *Journal of Communication Disorders* 30:457–75.

Meadow, K. 1968. Early manual communication in relation to the deaf child's intellectual, social, and communicative functioning. *American Annals of the Deaf* 113:24–41.

Meadow-Orlans, K. P. 1990. Research on developmental aspects of deafness. In *Educational and Developmental Aspects of Deafness*, eds. D. F. Moores and K. P. Meadow-Orlans. Washington, DC: Gallaudet University Press.

Mehl, A., and Thomson, V. 1998. Newborn hearing screening: The great omission. *Pediatrics* 101

Menyuk, P. 1974. Early development of receptive language: From babbling to words. In *Language Perspectives: Acquisition, Retardation, and Intervention*, eds. R. L. Schiefelbusch and L. L. Lloyd Baltimore, MD: University Park Press.

Menyuk, P., Lierbergott, J. W., and Schultz, M. C. 1995. *Early Language Development in Full-Term and Premature Infants.* Hillside, NJ: Lawrence Erlbaum Associates.

Miller, J. 1964. Institute for parents and their deaf children. *Volta Review* 66:185–97.

Miller, K. A. 1997. The status of the preschool deaf child. *American Annals of the Deaf* 142(3):53–59.

Mindel, E., and Vernon, M. 1971. *They Grow in Silence.* Silver Spring MD: National Association of the Deaf.

Miyamoto, R. T., Kirk, K. I., Robbins, A. M., Todd, S., and Riley, A. 1996. Speech perception and speech production skills with multichannel cochlear implants. *Acta Otolaryngology* (Stockh) 116:240–43.

Moeller, M. P., and Carney, A. E. 1993. Assessment and intervention with preschool hearing impaired children. In *Rehabilitative*

Audiology: Children and Adults, eds. J. G. Alpiner and P. A. McCarthy. Baltimore, MD: Williams and Wilkens

Moeller, M. P., and Condon, M. C. 1994. D.E.I.P.: A collaborative problem-solving approach to early intervention. In *Infants and Toddlers with Hearing Loss*, eds. J. Roush and N. D. Matkin. Timonium MD: York Press.

Moeller, M. P., Donaghy, K. F., Beauchaine, K. L., Lewis, D. E., and Stelmachowicz, P. G. 1996. Longitudinal study of FM system use in nonacademic settings: Effects on language development. *Ear and Hearing* 17:28–41.

Moog, A., and Geers, J. 1989. Factors predictive of the development of literacy in profoundly hearing-impaired adolescents. *Volta Review* 91(2):69–86.

Moog, J. S., Biedenstein, J. J., and Davidson, L. S. 1995. *SPICE: Speech Perception Instructional Curriculum and Evaluation*. St Louis, MO: Central Institute for the Deaf

Moores, D. F. 1992. What do we know and when did we know it? In *A Free Hand*, eds. M. Walworth, D. Moores, and T. O'Rorke. Silver Spring MD: T. J. Publishers.

Moores, D. F. 1996. *Educating the Deaf* (4th ed.). Boston: Houghton Mifflin Company.

Morgan, J. L. 1996. A rhythmic bias in preverbal speech segmentation. *Journal of Memory and Language* 35:666–82.

Morgan, J. L., and Saffran, J. R. 1995. Emerging integration of sequential and suprasegmental information in preverbal speech segmentation. *Child Development* 66:911–36.

Mueller, H. G., and Johnson R. 1979. The effects of various front-to-back ratios on the performance of directional microphone hearing aids. *Journal of the American Auditory Society* 5:30–34.

Munro, J., and Bach, T. 1975. Effects of time limited counseling on client change. *Journal of Counseling Psychology* 22:395–406.

Musselman, C., Wilson, A., and Lindsay, P. 1988. Effects of early intervention on hearing impaired children. *Exceptional Children* 55:222–28.

National Institute of Health. 1993. Early identification of hearing impairment in infants and young children. NIH Consensus Statement 11(1):1–25.

Nicholas, J. G., and Geers, A. E. 1997. Communication of oral deaf and normal hearing children at 36 months of age. *Journal of Speech Language And Hearing Research* 40:1314–27.

Nichols, G., and Ling, D. 1982. Cued speech and the reception of spoken language. *Journal of Speech and Hearing Research* 25:262–69.

Nienhuys, T. G., Horsborough, K. M., and Cross, T. G. 1985 Interaction between mothers and deaf or hearing children. *Applied Psycholinguistics* 6:121–39.

Ninio, A., and Bruner, J. 1978. The achievement and antecedents of labeling. *Journal of Child Language* 5:1–15.

Northern, J., and Downs, M. 1974. *Hearing in Children.* Baltimore: Williams and Wilkens.

Northern, J., and Hayes, D. 1994. Universal screening for infant hearing impairment: Necessary,beneficial, and justifiable. *Audiology Today* 6(2):1–3.

Oller, D. K. 1994. A synthetic model of infant vocal development. In *The Miami Cochlear Implant, Auditory & Tactile Skills Curriculum*, eds. K. C. Vergara and L. W . Miskiel. Miami: Intelligent Hearing Systems.

Oller, D. K., and Eilers, R. 1998. The role of audition in babbling. *Child Development* 59:441–49

Osberger, M. J. 1997A. Current issues in cochlear implants in children. *The Hearing Review* 4:28, 30–31.

Osberger, M. J. 1997B. Cochlear implantation in children under the age of two years: Candidacy considerations. *Otolaryngology - Head and Neck Surgery* 117(3): 145–49.

Osberger, M. J., Robbins, A. M., Todd, S. L., Riley, A., Kirk, K. I., and Carney, A. E. 1996. Cochlear implants and tactile aids for children with profound hearing impairment. In *Amplification for Children with Auditory Deficits*, eds. F. H. Bess, J. S. Gravel, and A. M. Tharpe. Nashville TN: Bill Wilkerson Center Press.

Osberger, M. J., Geier, L., Zimmerman-Phillips, S., and Barker, M. J. 1997. Use of parent-report scale to assess benefit in children given the Clarion cochlear implant. *The American Journal of Otology* 18(suppl): S79–S80.

Parasnis, I. 1983. Effects of parental deafness and early exposure to manual communication on the cognitive skills, English language skills, and field independence of young deaf adults. *Journal of Speech and Hearing Research* 26:588–94.

Parent, T. C., Chmiel, R., and Jerger, J. 1998. Comparison of performance with frequency transposition hearing aids and conventional hearing aids. *Journal of the American Academy of Audiology* 9(1):67–77.

Pollock, D. 1970. *Educational Audiology For the Limited Hearing Infant.* Springfield IL: Charles C Thomas.

Pollock, D. 1993. Reflections of a pioneer. *Volta Review* 95:197–204.

Prizant, B., and Wetherby, A. 1993. Communication and language assessment for young children. *Infants and Young Children* 5(4):20–34.

Quigley, S., and Paul, P. 1986. A perspective on academic achievement. In *Deafness in Perspective*, ed. D. Luterman. San Diego: College-Hill Press.

Robinette, M. E., and White, E. 1997.Top ten reasons universal newborn hearing screening should be the standard of care in the United States. *Audiology Today* 9(1):21.

Roeser, R.J. 1989.Tactile aids:Development issues and current status. In *Cochlear Implants in Young Deaf Children*, eds. E.Owens and D. K. Kessler. Boston: Little, Brown and Company.

Rogers, C. 1951. *Client Centered Therapy*. Boston: Houghton Mifflin Company.

Ross, M. 1992. Auditory capabilities of children with hearing impairment. In *Amplification for Children with Auditory Deficits*, eds. F. Bess, J. Gravel, and A. M. Tharpe. Nashville TN: Bill Wilkerson Center Press.

Ross, M. 1992. Implications of audiologic success. *Journal of American Academy of Audiology* 3:1–4.

Ross, M. 1997. A retrospective look at the future of aural rehabilitation. *Journal of the Academy of Rehabilitative Audiology* 30:11–26.

Roush, J. 1994, Strengthening family-professional relations: Advice from parents. In *Infants and Toddlers With Hearing Loss*, eds. J. Roush and N. D. Matkin. Baltimore, MD: York Press.

Rushmer, N., and Schuyler, P. 1994. Infant hearing resource. In *Infants and Toddlers with Hearing Loss*, eds. J. Roush and N. D. Matkin. Timonium MD: York Press.

Sabbeth, B., and Leventhal, J. 1988. Trial balloons: When families of ill children express needs in veiled ways. *Children's Health Care* 171:87–92.

Sacks, O. 1989. *Seeing Voices*. Berkeley and Los Angeles, CA: University of California Press.

Sandow, S., and Clark, D. B. 1977. Home intervention with parents of severely, subnormal preschool children: An interim report. *Child Care, Health, and Development* 4:29–39.

Schick, B., and Moeller, M. P. 1992. What is learnable in manually coded English sign systems? *Applied Linguistics* 13:313–40.

Schirmer, B. 1994. Language development and the goals of language instruction. In *Language and Literacy Developement in Children Who Are Deaf*. New York: Macmillian Publishing Co.

Schlesinger, H. 1986. Total communication in perspective. In *Deafness in Perspective*, ed. D. Luterman. San Diego: College-Hill Press.

Schlesinger, H. 1992. The elusive X factor: Parental contributions to literacy. In *A Free Hand*, eds. M. Walworth, D. Moores, and T. O'Rourke. Silver Spring MD: T. J. Publishers.

Schweitzer, C. 1997. Developments in digital hearing aids. *Trends in Amplification* 2(2):41–77.

Seewald, R. C. 1995. Universal habilitation. *American Journal of Audiology* 4:5.

Seewald R. C., and Ross, M. 1988. Amplification for young hearing-impaired children. In *Amplification for Children with Auditory Deficits*, ed. M. C. Pollack. Orlando FL: Grune and Stratton.

Seewald, R. C., Moodie, K. S., Sinclair, S. T., and Cornelisse, L. E. 1996. Traditional and Theoretical approaches to selecting amplification for infants and young children. In *Amplification for Children with Auditory Deficits*, eds. F. H. Bess, J. S. Gravel, and A. M. Tharpe. Nashville TN: Bill Wilkerson Center Press.

Sehgal, S. T., Kirk, K. I., Svirshy, M., and Miyamoto, R. T. 1998. The effects of processor strategy on the speech perception performance of pediatric Nucleus multichannel cochlear implant users. *Ear and Hearing* 19(2):149–61.

Shapiro, E. 1994. *Grief As a Family Process.* New York: Guilford Press.

Skinner, N.W., Clark, G. M., Whitford, L. A., Seligman, P. M., Staller, S. J., Shipp, D. B., Shallop, J. K., Everingham, C., Manapace, C. M., Arndt, P. L., Antogenelli, T., Brimacomb, J. A., Pijl, S., Daniels, P., George, C. R., McDermott, H. J., and Beiter, A. L. 1994. Evaluation of a new spectral peak (SPEAK) strategy for the Nuclius 22 channel cochlear implant system. *American Journal of Otology* 15 (Supplement 2):15–27.

Smith, A. D., Pictor, P., Edwards, C., Goodman, J. T., and McMurray, B. 1985.The crib-o-gram in the NICU: An evaluation based on brainstem electric response audiometry. *Ear and Hearing* 6:20–24.

Snow, C. 1977. The development of conversation between mothers and babies. *Journal of Child Language* 4:1–22.

Snow, C., Dubber, C., and DeBlauw, A. 1982. Routines in mother-child interaction. In *The Language of Poverty*, eds. L Feajans and P. C. Farraru. New York: Academic Press.

Spencer, P. E., and Gutfreund, M. K. 1990. Directiveness in mother-infant interactions. In *Educational and Developmental Aspects of Deafness*, eds. D. F. Moores and K. P. Meadow-Orlans. Washington, DC: Gallaudet University Press.

Staab, W. J. and Lybarger, S. F. 1994. Characteristics and use of hearing aids. In *Handbook of Clinical Audiology*, ed. J. Katz.Baltimore MD: Williams and Wilkins.

Stark, R. E. 1991. Speech-language habilitation of hearing-impaired children: Basis for assessment and training. *American Journal of Otology* 12 Suppl:62–66.

Stark, R. E., Bernstein, L. E., and De Morest, M. E. 1993. Vocal communication in the first 18 months of life. *Journal of Speech Language and Hearing Research* 36:548–58.

Stelmachowicz, P. G., Kalberer, A., and Lewis, D. E. 1996. Situational hearing aid response profile (SHARP). In *Amplification for Children with Auditory Deficits*, eds. F. H. Bess, J. S. Gravel, and A. M. Tharpe. Nashville TN: Bill Wilkerson Center Press.

Stewart, D. 1993. Bi-Bi to MCE? *American Annals of the Deaf* 138(4):331–37.

Stoel-Gammon, C. 1998. Role of babbling and phonology in early linguistic development. In *Transitions in Prelinguistic Communication*, eds. A. M.. Wetherby, S. F. Warren, and J. Reichle, Baltimore, MD: Paul H. Brookes Publishing Co.

Stuckless, E. R., and Birch, J. 1966. The influence of early manual communication on the linguistic development of deaf children. *American Annals of the Deaf* 111:452–60.

Swisher, M. V., and Thomson, M. 1985. Mothers learning simultaneous communication: The dimensions of the task. *American Annals of the Deaf* 135:212–20.

Tharpe, A. M., and Clayton, E. W. 1997. Newborn hearing screening: Issues in legal liability and quality assurance. *American Journal of Audiology* 6(2):5–12.

The Pediatric Working Group of the Conference on Amplification for Children With Auditory Deficits 1996. Amplification for infants and children with hearing loss. *American Journal of Audiology* 5(1): 53–68.

Thompson, M. 1994. ECHI, The University of Washington, Seattle. In *Infants and Toddlers with Hearing Loss*, eds. J. Roush and N. D. Matkin. Timonium MD: York Press.

Tracy, S. 1960. The Tracy Clinic. In *The Modern Educational Treatment of Deafness*, ed. Sir Alexander Ewing. Manchester: The University of Manchester Press.

Vernon, M., and Koh, S. D. 1971. Effects of oral pre-preschool compared to early manual communication on education and communication in deaf children. *American Annals of the Deaf* 116:569–74.

Tyler, R. S., Fryauf-Bertschy, H., Kelsay, D. M., Gantz, B. J., Woodworth, G. P., and Parkinson, A. 1996. Speech perception by prelingually deaf children using cochlear implants. *Otolaryngology - Head and Neck Surgery* 117(3): 180–87.

Vihman, M. 1998. Early phonological development. In *Articulation and Phonological Disorders*. eds. J. E. Bernthal and N. Bankson. Boston: Allyn and Bacon.

Warren, S. F., and Yoder, P. J. 1998. Transition from preintentional to intentional communication. In *Transitions in*

Prelinguistic Communication, eds. A. M. Wetherby, S. F. Warren, and J. Reichle, Baltimore, MD: Paul H. Brookes Publishing Co.

Watkins, S. 1987. Long term effects of home intervention with hearing impaired children. *American Annals of the Deaf* 132:267–71.

Waxman, R. P., and Spencer, P. E. 1997. What mothers do to support infant visual attention: Sensitivities to age and hearing status. *Journal of Deaf Studies and Deaf Education* 2(2):104–14.

Webster, E. 1977. *Counseling with Parents of Handicapped Children*. New York: Grune and Stratton.

Westby, C. E. 1988. Children's play: Reflections on social competence. *Seminars in Speech and Language* 9:1–14.

Wetherby, A. M., Yonclas, D. G., and Bryden, A. A. 1989. Communicative profiles of preschool children with handicaps: Implications for early identification. *Journal of Speech Language and Hearing Research* 54:148–58.

White, K. R., and Maxon, A. B. 1995. Universal screening for infant hearing impairment; simple, beneficial, and presently justified. *International Journal of Pediatric Otorhinolaryngology* 32:201–11.

Wilbur, R. 1976. The linguistics of manual languages and manual systems. In *Communication Assessment and Intervention Strategies*, ed. L. Lloyd. Baltimore: University Park Press.

Wilcox, M. J., and Shannon, M. S. 1998. Facilitating the transition from prelinguistic to linguistic communication. In *Transitions in Prelinguistic Communication*, eds. A. M. Wetherby, S. F. Warren, and J. Reichle. Baltimore, MD: Paul H. Brookes Publishing Co.

Winefield, R. 1987. *Never the Twain Shall Meet*. Washington, DC: Gallaudet University Press.

Winton, P. J., and Bailey, Jr., D. B. 1994. Becoming family centered: Strategies for self-examination. In *Infants and Toddlers With Hearing Loss*, eds. J. Roush and N. D. Matkin. Baltimore, MD: York Press.

Yoshinaga-Itano, C. 1997. Factors predictive of successful outcomes of deaf and hard-of-hearing children of hearing parents. Paper presented at the meeting of the National Deafness and Other Communication Disorders Advisory Council, Bethesda MD.

Yoshinaga-Itano, C., and Stredler-Brown, A. 1992. Learning to communicate: Babies with hearing impairments make their needs known. *Volta Review* 95:107–29.

Yoshinaga-Itano, C., Apuzzo, M., Coulter, D., and Stredler-Brown, A. 1996. The effect of early identification of hearing loss on developmental outcomes. Paper presented at the Third Annual Infant Hearing Screening Seminar, Providence, RI.

Index

*(Page numbers in italics indi-
acte materials in illustrations.)*

Activity-making sounds,
140–42
Americans with Disabilities
Act, 27–28
American School for the Deaf,
3, 12
American Sign Language
(ASL), 18–19, 30–31
Amplification, 16, 17, 19; in educating deaf children, 25–26;
for infants, 126–27
Amplification options, *152*; alternatives to conventional
amplification and, 166
Animal noises as stimuli in auditory therapy, 112–13,
128–29
Arehart, K. H., 176, 177
Articulation training, 6
Assimilation into hearing society, 32–33. *See also*
Mainstreamed deaf students
Assistive hearing technologies,
149–52; cochlear implants,
168–72; FM systems,
163–64; frequency transposition devices, 164, 166–68;
hearing aid developments,
175–84; issues in application

of, 175–84; matching to children's needs, 179–84; tactile
aids, 172–75
Audiologists, 12; selecting and
fitting practices of pediatric,
178, 182
Audiometers, 12
Auditory brainstem response
(ABR) testing, 37–38, 43, 44,
75
Auditory/Oral approach, 15,
16–17
Auditory therapy and training,
17, 111–12, 113–15, 127–29;
early, 147
Auralism, 15–16, 30
AVR Sonovation, 167

Babbidge, H. S., 13–14
Babies' intentional communica-
tion, 142–43
Baby games, 134. *See also* Play
Baby's signals and communica-
tive behavior, adult re-
sponses to, 91
Bell, A. G., 5, 6–9
Bell, M., 6–7
Bender, R., 2, 4, 7, 11
Bess, F., 40–41, 178, 182
Bi-lingual/bicultural approach
(Bi-Bi), 15, 18–20, 28–30
Birch, J., 14, 21

Bodner-Johnson, B., 26
Book reading routines, 142–43
Boothroyd, A., 183–84

Caregivers: communication
   with deaf baby and, 109; influence of (on development of
   communication), 90–93;
   stages of language develop-
   ment taught to, 124; use of
   gestures by, 124–25. *See also*
   Parents
Carhart, R., 12
Carney, A., 36
Central Institute for the Deaf
   (C.I.D.). 13, 17
Clarke School for the Deaf, 5,
   11, 17, 60
Cochlear implants, 32
Columbia Institute for the Deaf
   and Dumb, 5
Communication: early development of, 89–93; exposure to
   manual, 14; total, 6; visual
   system of, 20
Compression amplification, 153
Compression threshold, 153
Condon, M. C., 63
Cooing/reactive sound making,
   140
Cornett, R. O., 20
Counseling, 187–96; coping
   with grief and, 204–208; pit-
   falls of, 200–204; responding
   to parents and, 198, 208–13;
   techniques of, 196–200; time
   limits in, 213
Cued speech approach, 15, 20–21

Deaf children: approaches to
   educating, 15–21; auditory
   training for, 111–12; communication goals of, 109; needs
   of (for development of oral
   language), 86; passivity of,

109; predictor of literacy for,
   26; research on teaching of,
   21–27; speech therapy for,
   111, 129–31
Deaf clubs, 28
Deafness, 18; risk factors for (in
   neonates), 38–39. *See also*
   Early detection and inter-
   vention
Deafness management scale (D.
   M>Q), 23
Deaf people, isolation of, 8
Deaf students, mainstreamed,
   25
Demonstration home projects,
   62
DigiVoc®, 173
Directional microphones, 158

Early detection and intervention, 49–54; cost of, 45–46;
   feasibility of, 40–42; methods for, 32–39; problems
   with, 36–37, 40–41, 42–45,
   47–48; results of, 35; timing
   of, 48–50
Education of deaf children,
   14,15; auditory-oral approach, 15, 16–17; auditory-
   verbal approach, 15–16;
   early pre-school, 12–13. *See
   also* Parent education
Educational achievement, factors in deaf students', 26–27
Emerson College program,
   63–71, 71–77, 77–84
Emerson nursery, 31, 65–67
English as a second language,
   19
Environmental sounds for early
   auditory training, 112–13,
   128–29
Erting, C., 18–19
Evoked Otoacoustic Emission
   (EOAE), 39, 43, 44

Family-centered intervention programs, 77, 88
Family needs, 86–87
First words, 143–44
FM systems, 163–65; boot receiver of, *165*; receiver audio shoe, *165*; reduction in size of, 164. *See also* Hearing aids
Frequency Transposition Devices, 164, 166–68. *See also* Hearing aids

Gallaudet College (University), 5, 18; first deaf president of, 19
Gallaudet, E. M., 5–6, 8, 9
Gallaudet, T. H., 1, 2
Goldstein, M., 11, 15
Grandparents, 72–73

Hayes, D, 41
Hearing aids, 7–8; background noise and, 157–59; button type, 149; in children in schools for the deaf, 26; children who discontinue use of, 150; compression circuits in, 155; developments in, 152–63; digital signal processing (DSP) type of, 161–63; directional microphones and, 158; for infants, 126–27; input compression type of, 154–55; manual volume control of, 155; microphone designs in, 158–60; multichannel type of, 155–57; multi-microphone technology and, 157–60; omnidirectional microphone in, 158; transposition type of, 167–68; vacuum tube, 12; wide-dynamic range (WDRC) type of, 155. *See also* FM systems

Hedley-Williams, A., 178, 182
Horace Mann School, 7
Hubbard, G., 3–4

Infant communicative capacities, *96–98*; impact of deafness on, 197–110; social context and development of, 105–106; speech perception and, 93–95, 102, 103; stages in, 95, 99–105; vocal development and, *96–98*, 99–105
Infants, obtaining valid performance measures on, 179–80. *See also* Deaf children
Input compression hearing aids, 154–55
Intervention: factors that might delay, 177; initial stages of, 147; new model for, 116–19, *120*, 121–36, *137–39*, 140–48. *See also* Early detection and intervention
Intervention and management programs, 55, 71–77; admission to (Emerson program), 77; center-based, 61–65; deaf parents and, 79–81; at Emerson College, 63–84; family-centered, 77; focusing on parents and, 81; funding for, 81; grandparents in, 72–73; intense short-term, 60–61; itinerent, 55–60; nursery, 65–67; parents and, 56–57, 59–60, 61, 62, 64, 66, 67–71, 74–76, 81–82; special features in (Emerson College), 71–77; special issues in (Emerson College), 77–84; staffing, 83–84; support group for parents in, 68–71; therapy in, 67–68

Johnson, R. E., 18–19

Kneepoint, 153
Koh, S. D., 21

Language-learning environment, model to create a, 145–47
Learning vacations, 60–61
Liddell, S., 18–19
Ling, D., 16, 20
Linguistic development of deaf children, 14
Lip reading, 6, 17, 20
Listening experiences, 129

Mainstreamed deaf students, 24–25, 31, 32
Mainstreaming, PL 94–142 and, 28
Manualists, 1
Manual language system, 2, 3
Maternal self-esteem, significance of, 27
Matkin, N. D., 55
Maxon, A. B., 41–42
Meadow, K., 21
Miller, K. A., 10–11
Mindel, E., 15
Moeller, M. P., 36, 63
Moores, D. F., 21, 32–33

Newborns: high-risk register for, 38, 39, 42, 46; intervention and referral for deaf, 41, 45; screening, 37, 40, 42–45, 75; universal deafness screening for, 40–42
Nichols, G., 20
Northern, J., 41

"Oops" games, 141–42
Oralism, 3, 4, 9–10, 13; emotional effects of failed, 15
Oralists, 1
Osberger, M. J., 174–75
Otoacoustic emission testing, 39, 43, 44

Paradise, J., 40–41
Parasnis, I., 22
Parent education, 13
Parent facilitators, 58
Parent-infant interactions and routines: for intervention, 131–36, *137–39*, 140–45; early, 146–47
Parent-to-parent contact and communication, 59–60
Parents, 64, 84; clinicians and, 88; counseling of, 187, 196–204; deaf, 21–22, 79–81, 108; dependence on therapists by, 57; empowering to help children, 31–32; experienced (as mentors and tutors), 59; in family-centered programs, 88; feelings of, 187–88, 188–96; hearing, 19, 22, 79–80; involvement of, 16, 25, 26, 67–68; responses of (to baby's communicative behavior), 91–92; responses of (to child's deafness), 21–22, 108; results of infant screening tests and, 43, 46, 47–50, 51, 53–54; support groups for, 68–71, 79–80; underutilization of, 25. *See also* Caregivers
Phonak Microlink® FM system, 164
Phonic Ear Free Ear®, 164
Phonological development, beginning of delays in, 141
Play, 131–36, child's speech development and, 105–106
PL 94–142 (Americans with Disabilities Act), 27–28
Pollock, D., 16

Repetitive sounds, use of, 141
Residual hearing, 12
Rogers, C., 196–98, 210

Ross, M., 25–26, 33
Rouse, J., 55

Schools for the deaf: probable future of, 27; superior achieving students in, 24; teachers in early, 8. *See also names of specific schools*
Screening, 176; high-risk register and, 38, 39, 42, 46; risk factors and, 38–39. *See also* Early detection and intervention; Newborns
Signing, 8, 9–10, 13, 86; effects of early , 22; effects of judicious use of, 31
Sign system, 2. *See also* American Sign Language (ASL); Manual language system
Speech, 19
Speech perception by infants, 93–95, *96–98*, 102
Speech therapy, 111, 129–31
Stuckless, E. R., 14, 21

Tactaid®, 173
Tactile aids, 172–75

Teachers of the deaf, 8, 10–13, 15, 83–84
Telex Select® 2-40FM BTE, 164
Tharpe, A. M., 178, 182
Total communication (TC), 6, 15, 17–18; assignment to programs using, 23
TranSonic® frequency transposition hearing aid, 167–68

Unitron Industries/AVR Communications Unicom® System, 164

Vernon, M., 15, 21
Vocalization, encouraging, 130–31

Webster, E., 198–99
White, K. R., 41–42
Wide-dynamic range compression (WDRC) hearing aids, 155
Written English, acquisition of, 14